30

TEMIDAYO OLANIPEKUN

First Edition November 2020

Manufactured in the United States of America

Published by E4H Media, Houston, Texas

ISBN: 978-1-7355738-3-0

Dedication

To my husband Titilope Olanipekun, my love, soulmate and devoted father to our son, thank you for a life filled with true happiness, contentment and the motive to become a better person everyday. With your rock-solid support, I know I can face anything in life. I will forever cherish your precious love.

To my son Tamilore Nathaniel Olanipekun, thank you for awakening a newly found depth of gratitude and compassion within me. You brighten up my world effortlessly.

To my Parents, Kolawole and Omowunmi Kola-Kehinde, thank you for your unconditional love, for believing in me, for instilling the right values within me and giving me the life every child deserves.

To my brother Onaopemipo Kola-Kehinde, thank you for being that piece of childhood that can never be lost, filled with laughter, stories and cherished moments. You are the best brother a proud sister could ask for.

Challenge Yourself 

As you dive into this Book, challenge yourself with this 30 Day Challenge geared toward daily improvements in your professional and personal life.

- Day 1: Put one thing that makes you happy in your office.
- Day 2: Pick out 3 things you currently own and donate them.
- Day 3: Sign up for a professional certification that improves a skill relevant to your industry.
- Day 4: Design a morning and evening routine.
- Day 5: Give a compliment to yourself and a colleague.
- Day 6: Wake up 1 hour earlier than usual.
- Day 7: Read about the impact of your industry in the country you live in and in one country you currently do not reside in.
- Day 8: Design a priority list for the day.
- Day 9: Plan a stay-cation or vacation sometime this year.
- Day 10: Register for a conference related to your industry.
- Day 11: Go to a place you have never been before or take a route you have never taken before.
- Day 12: Write a letter to your future self.
- Day 13: Spend 30 minutes learning a foreign language.
- Day 14: Take at least 10,000 steps in a day.
- Day 15: Listen and dance to your favorite music.
- Day 16: Volunteer with a cause that helps others.
- Day 17: Watch a documentary about your industry.
- Day 18: Prepare 7 outfits for the next 7 days in advance.
- Day 19: Teach something you do well to someone it can benefit.
- Day 20: Give your partner genuine reasons why you are grateful for him or her.
- Day 21: Declutter your email inbox.
- Day 22: Start a Journal.
- Day 23: Watch a Ted Talk video.
- Day 24: Try a new food recipe.
- Day 25: Share an insightful article.
- Day 26: Incorporate at least 1 hour of 'me' or 'think' time into your daily routine.
- Day 27: Design a budget.
- Day 28: Listen to a new podcast.
- Day 29: Eat at least one meal as a family.
- Day 30: Learn 30 new words.

Contents

Preface

Inspired by my 30th birthday in the midst of the soaring unemployment rate during the Coronavirus pandemic, 30 features a reflection on tactics that helped me succeed over different stages of my career, from college as a Student, to the workforce as a Professional in corporate America. Grounded in designing a purpose-centric career built around your calling, this practical guide walks through how to find the next opportunity, a clear understanding of the current state of your career, unveiling your "why", discovering your career destination, setting goals, developing goal achieving strategies, keying into the power of mentorship and exploring the act of seizing opportunities. Essentially, the overarching objective of this book is to fortify career dreams, aspirations and help 30 million career goals become reality.

Whether you are in search of your next opportunity, a goal achieving strategy or essential tips on developing a fulfilling career, this book will lead you on track to believing in your abilities with a strategy in hand. It is my hope that you will find this book useful and recommend it to anyone that can benefit from the contents. Stories of individuals who have lost opportunities due to the economic impact of COVID-19 are highlighted in order to help them find the next opportunity. When you go through these stories, please pay special attention. My goal is to inspire you to not just stop with these individuals but also make a constant effort to look within your network and find job seekers you can be of help to. Even if you do not have an opportunity to offer, giving career advice or helping a job seeker review a resume goes a long way.

Visit www.temidayoolanipekun.com to find out other ways to get involved or submit a story along with a resume as a job seeker.

Acknowledgements

Dear family, friends and coworkers, thank you for shaping me into the person I am today. Writing this book has been more rewarding than I could have envisioned. None of which would have been possible without the interactions, conversations and lessons learned over the past three decades. Whether you have been there since birth or we crossed paths due to destiny, school, sports, work, conferences, nonprofit organizations or events, thank you for making an impact in my life, no matter how big or small. Thank you for allowing me to be a part of your life in some way and giving me something to think or smile about. To the following individuals, listed in alphabetical order by last name, I extend my sincere thanks.

Adetola Abatan
Danait Abraha
Nathan Adams
Adeyemi Adebayo
Folashade Adebayo
Oluwaseun Adeola
Mofesola Adeola
Omotola Adeoti
Tayo Adereni
Bunmi Adetutu
Dayo Adeyefa
Kemi Adeyemi
Abenaa Adjei
Chidinma Aham-Neze
Julia Akinboyewa
Gbenga Akinde
Yetunde Akinde
Adeola Akinfaderin

Vincent Akinola
Adedoyin Alabi
Busayo Alade
Ayo Alaiyegbami
Bami Alao
Femi Alao
Mayo Alao
Gwen Allain
Aisha Almaazmi
Veronica Andrade
Nnenna Aneto
Ana Karina Araujo
Jide Arije
Yinka Arije
Irvin Arreola
Soji Awe
Lola Awodola
James Ayodele
Gayathri Baburaj
Emma Baldisserotto
Kristina Barth
Dean Bendele
Kiera Benson
Tosin Bewaji
Joy Blevins
Matthew Blomerth
Stefan Boettcher
Joseph Bonner
Irina Borovskaya
Jason Brien
Lauri Burke
Sterling Carter
Leon Cassidy
Meagan Chang
Emily Clark
Irene Cornell-Ade
Cornelius Cornell-Ade
Shara Cutts
Omolayo Dada
David Dexter
Obinna Duru
Nina Ebiteh
Bayo Edun
Lanre Edun
Joffi Effoe
Valery Effoe
Jesse Einhorn
Breah Elizabeth
Sherif Elkhatib
Rhiannon Ellifritz
Jasmin Espy
Alfred Eustes
Ashlei Evans
Kingsley Ewetuya
Tolu Ewherido
Femi Fadeyi
Yasmine Faied
Femi Felix-Ukwu
Libby Felts
William Fleckenstein
Sulaiman Folarin
Segun Forahunbi
Steven Foster
Jason Fung
Sunil Garg
Folajimi Gbadamosi

Shewaga Gebre-Michael
Helen Godfrey
Lemuel Godinez
Gustavo Gomez
Tanya Gordon
Adrian Michael Green
Elyse Grimes
Filmon Habtemichael
David Hampton
Lillie Hayes
Nima Heydarian
Todd Hoffman
Christopher Hoo
Mael Houndjahoue
Zille Humayun
Efehi Igbinomwanhia
Uchenna Igbokwe
Melanie Igwe
Uchenna Ikediobi
Istifa Ikenyei
Temidayo Kifuliat Ishola
Denise Jacinto
Christal Jackson
Thalia Jaguande
Jenna Jakovich
Abby Jayeola
Anjali Jha
Lenay Johnson
Ayo Jones
Karim Jones
Francine Kabongo
Jomon Kannala
Moji Karimi
Gary Katz
Amanuel Kb
Kolawole Kehinde
Kosenatu Ejire Kehinde
Omowunmi Kola-Kehinde
Onaopemipo Kola-Kehinde
Sameer Ketkar
Mani Khaghani
Gerald Kimani
Sunil Kini
Melissa Knight
Steven Koch
Abby Kotun
Igor Kuvaev
Femi Lawson
Ezinne Lawson
Yuechen Li
Neil Little
Faye Liu
Nelly Lopez
Taylor Lowe
Ali Al Macki
Kavita Manak
Emil Marinov
Isabel Mazingo
Andrew McAndrew
Carrie McClelland
Regina Mellinger
Ricardo Mendez
Bill Mercer
Mark Miller
Stella Misomali
Oscar Mora

Shari Moreno
Ruqaiya Muhammad
Efren Munoz
Wambui Mutoru
Kamwana Mwara
Ankit Nagpal
Marian Newman
Tan Ngo
Chibuike Njoku
Nii Nunoo
Chika Nwankwo
Fiemu Nwariaku
Ndidi Obaji
Nkechi Odumodu
Ike Ogbaa
Oluwaseun Ogungbenle
Tunde Ogunjobi
Chimuanya Okoli
Chike Okoye
Chinelo Okoye-Mbakogu
Kemi Olafusi-Akinrinola
Kunleola Musiliu Olakehinde
Ifedayo Olanipekun
Olajumoke Olanipekun
Oluwafemi Olanipekun
Oluwaseun Olanipekun
Oluwatosin Olanipekun
Tamilore Nathaniel Olanipekun
Titilope Olanipekun
Ola Olanipekun
Omolola Olanipekun
Olalekan Olanipekun
Isi Olanipekun
Isioma Joyce Oleleh
Seun Olotu
Olaotan Olowofela
Liz Olubodun
Ayokunle Omoyeni
Damilola Omoyeni
Kunle Orogbemi
Ayo Owolabi
Bukky Owolabi
Funmi Oyatogun
Seun Oyatogun
Blessing Oyeniyi
Robert Pelley
Ashling Petro-Roy
Brooke Pierce
Denis Pone
Paul Povel
Shrenik Ramani
Erin Reed
Saul Rivera
Larry Rogers
Carelia Rojas
Annie Rose
Prashanth Sabbineni
Ramy Saleh
Supitcha Samart
Al Sami
Benjamin Sanchez
Alejandro Sanoja
Vanessa Scobie
Arianna Scott
Halee Scott
Sharoma Scurry-Graves

Raphael Serrano
Ahmed Shedeed
Ayomide Shittu
Mudassir Siddiqui
Jahi Simbai
Raju Sitaula
Livia Sivila
Jeb Smartt
Delisa Somoye
Steve Sonnenberg
Fummy Sotunde
Jake Stein
James Sullivan
Murat Syzdykov
Seyi Taiwo
Olasumbo Taiwo
Douglas Tamashiro
Ariel Thomas
Shina Tomori
David Tonner
Francis Ujeyah
Khanh Vu
Miriam Walker
Gavin Wall
Alexander Wallace
Carlos Wallace
Quinta Warren
Robert Wichert
Jenny Wu
Tosin Yusuf

30

Dear Job Seeker

It is normal to get perturbed about a job loss, especially during a pandemic like COVID-19 with multifaceted uncertainties. Hiring freezes, the savings account tanking, millions unemployed, studies indicating decade long economic impacts; it is a frightening period without an end in sight. Considering these complications along with worrying about the health and safety of your family, it is definitely okay not to be fine.

Allow yourself the right to decompress and come to terms with the situation. However, do not allow yourself to get so consumed with grief that it erodes every sense of motivation. Negative thoughts will have no effect on boosting your job search efforts or interview process, so find it within you to remember this is not your fault and millions just like you are facing the same situation. Though the extent of the challenges ahead is unknown, when the fear of the unknown creeps in, remind yourself that you survived till this point and you are capable of rebuilding your world post COVID-19. Below is my take on the five key important elements as you search for the next opportunity.

Cover Letter

A cover letter is a chance to tell your story and express your personality in a way no other application document can. It solidifies your candidacy by giving the employer an insight into the reason why you are the best candidate for the job. Always see a cover letter as a vital part of your application unless an employer specifically tells you not to include one. Below is a template to use on your job search journey.

Dear <Recruiter's Name>,

I am pleased to submit my application for the <Position> at <Organization>. As an applicant with vast experience in <Job Skills>, my experience and educational background aligns well with this role. I have demonstrated my capability throughout my career with top accomplishments such as <top 3 accomplishments>. My passion for the <Industry Name> stems from <Your Why, Your Calling, Your Purpose>. <Organization> has proven itself as an expert in this field and <Other Reasons Why the Organization is of Interest>. The alignment between my mission in life and <Organization's> mission will further instill the highest level of service and devotion to your organization.

I am highly enthusiastic about the possibility of being part of <Organization's> continued success and offer my resume for review. I strongly believe my drive, values and experience would make me a valuable asset to your team. I am eager to receive your feedback. Thank you for reviewing my application.

Sincerely,
<Your Name>

Resume

A resume serves to justify why you are a competitive applicant and why you should be given the opportunity to interview for the position of interest. It should be succinct and leave the employer with a conviction to want to get to know you better as an applicant. A resume is typically screened for less than 30 seconds before the decision is made to dive in deeper or move on to the next candidate. Below are 6 tips for encouraging an employer to dive in deeper.

- The most important element on your resume is your contact information, which allows an employer the ability to follow-up with you. Your contact information should be placed at the top of your resume with your name, phone number and email at the minimum.

- The key information prospective employers look for on your resume in order to determine if you meet the requirements for an interview are your educational background and your employment history. Your start and end dates as well as your degrees, job titles and the names of the organizations you have worked with should be easily found on the resume.
- Aim to make the resume appealing in appearance to help the employer digest the information better. To achieve this, use a resume template that provides sufficient white space, standard margins and a legible font size.
- List your most impactful experiences with quantified accomplishments. To give you an example, within the next sentence, think of the option that showcases you as a stronger candidate. I led an initiative, which grew the company revenue, or I led a team of 20 analysts, which grew the company revenue by 85% within 4 months. The metrics within the second option stands out better and demonstrates credibility by

showing your ability to track progress.

- Unemployment bias is the notion that being unemployed for too long leads to outdated skills. This bias makes it harder to get a job. It is therefore important to reduce unemployment gaps within your resume. The best gap filler is an opportunity that would expand your expertise in your field. Volunteer with organizations that focus on causes within your field, pursue a new degree or sign up for a workshop. Essentially, avoid gaps by getting involved in productive activities that can improve desired skills and be included in your resume.
- After fine-tuning your resume, have it reviewed by at least two recruiters and two professionals within your industry of interest. This ensures that the resume successfully conveys a sense of professionalism, portrays you as a strong candidate and includes keywords that employers and applicant tracking system algorithms look for when vetting candidates.

Job Search

This is usually the most daunting part. When job searching, it is good to start by applying to positions through job boards, industry associations and actual company websites. The most effective way to find a job, however, is to tap into your network. By your network, I am referring to your family, friends, industry peers, school and corporate alumni network, former professors and managers, academic and career advisors. With tens of millions of individuals currently looking for employment opportunities, a direct recommendation to either a job or someone within an organization usually goes a long way.

A good approach to utilizing your network is to make a list of 200 people within your industry of interest and prioritize the list based on your judgment of an individual's willingness and ability to help. Reach out to everyone starting from the end of the list, which allows practice and helps you prepare first before moving towards the top candidates. Practice with about 10 individuals at the bottom of your list to develop an effective networking pitch that works for you. Then, move to the top of your list and work your way down the list. When reaching out to each individual, be sincere and clear about the reason for reaching out but focus more on sharing your story, asking for advice and generating real conversations. Regardless of the outcome of each contact, always show appreciation. If you exhaust the initial list without any main lead, repeat the steps with a new list. If you run out of a list of people you already know, build a new list by connecting with new people within your field of interest through continuous development opportunities. You can take an industry related course, volunteer to work with an organization with a similar cause to yours, network on LinkedIn and other professional network platforms. Lead with your enthusiasm for your industry and you might just stumble upon individuals that will introduce you to the next opportunity.

Interview

I have always prepared for interviews as if each one was the most important examination of my life. The success of an interview has as much to do with preparation as it does your ability to convey the values you hope to create for the organization during the interview. Give the preparation process your best effort.

- Have informational interviews with people that already work within the organization you will be interviewing with.

- Read through the company's financial statements, listen to earning calls and master viable ways to maximize shareholders' value.
- Familiarize yourself thoroughly with the company's management team, main competitors, line of businesses and the role you are applying for.
- Check the company website and social media accounts on a regular basis for updates.
- Get a sense of the corporate culture in order to dress appropriately to the interview.

During the interview, your goal is to show your ability to add value to the company, show that you believe the company is a good fit for you and show that you are capable of working well with others. Remember the often forgotten but arguably the most important part of an interview, your attitude. Even though your educational background and experience are important to a potential employer, walking into the interview with a negative demeanor can sabotage the interview before it begins. It is important to lead with a positive attitude and aim to make this second nature by the time for the interview. Set aside time to stay positive daily. My favorite positivity boosters are exercising, cultivating gratitude and listening to positive music. Find out activities that help you stay positive and incorporate them into your daily routine.

The hiring process does not end with the completion of an interview. It is important to follow-up with the prospective employer to convey an unwavering interest in the job. Put yourself in the shoes of a hiring manager and imagine two candidates with the same educational background, work experience and level of performance during the interview. If one candidate follows up after the interview process and the other does not, whom would you most likely select for the job? Following up with a thank you note will take a small fraction of the time spent on the entire job search and interview process. Do not hurt your chances of landing your dream job by overlooking this simple, yet paramount part of an interview process.

Persistence

Finding the next opportunity in a post COVID-19 world will be quite daunting. Now more than ever, the relentless commitment to persistence is vital despite oppositions. Regardless of the rejection letters and unsuccessful interviews that might come, it is important to remain diligent through continuous effort that will lead to success in the long run.

A good way to remain persistent is to treat the process like a full-time job by managing time effectively based on the priority level of each activity within the process. A calendar is a must during this process. Apart from using calendars to schedule events and meetings, they are great for allotting time to tasks. Rather than just having it in mind to research target companies for example, block an hour daily within your calendar. Instead of just making notes of tasks to accomplish, label the notes with specific due times and dates for easy organization. A note to connect with 5 recruiters per day is good, but the same note linked to a reminder every weekday at 2 pm increases the likelihood of staying persistent.

Opportunity does not favor the unprepared.
When one door of opportunity closes, another one will eventually open so stay prepared during your search. For every unsuccessful ending along the process, extract the lesson learned, move on quickly and actively seek opportunities out. When the next opportunity comes along, in order to translate that opportunity into a purposeful career, it is necessary to unleash your full

potential, which is what the rest of this book is focused on.

Career Diagnosis

In order to cultivate a purposeful career, you must first evaluate where you are currently. At the first thought of it, where you are currently might seem like an easy answer. The first thing that comes to mind is the job title that is currently held or the level of experience within the industry of interest. The answer is not that simple however.

When building a house, the foundation is built first to form the base upon which the house will stand for years. No matter how strong a house is, when accompanied with a weak foundation, the entire structure can crumble easily. Just as a strong foundation is mandatory for the long-term stability of a house, a solid understanding of where you currently are within your career will provide the ability to adequately navigate your career.

A personal SWOT analysis is a great tool for understanding where you are currently. The acronym SWOT stands for Strengths, Weaknesses, Opportunities and Threats; together, the analysis serves as a strategic planning technique for assessing these four elements. Essentially, the analysis allows the ability to unveil what you are good at, potential pitfalls you are most susceptible to, how to leverage your skills to tap into available opportunities and how to manage risks in order to plan ahead for potential threats.

To begin the analysis, personally evaluate what your Strengths, Weaknesses, Opportunities and Threats are relative to your industry. Then seek the same evaluation from your professional peers and bosses because the wrong perception can be career hindering in the long-term. The evaluation from your point of view as well as others provides the opportunity to see yourself as others see you and reevaluate attributes whereby self-perception differs from others' perception. Based on the combined evaluation, go through the questions below and list out the top answers.

Internal Strengths

What skills are you naturally good at, which set you apart from others and can be of benefit to your career?

____
____
____
____
____
____

Internal Weaknesses

What habits do you possess that can negatively impact your career?

____

____

____

____

____

____

External Opportunities

What external factors currently exist within your industry, which can be leveraged for growth along your career path?

____

____

____

____

____

____

External Threats

What are external factors within your industry that can jeopardize your career?

____

____

____

____

____

____

What actions can you take to leverage your internal strengths and external opportunities?

____

____

____

____

____

____

What actions can you take to minimize your internal weaknesses and external threats?

____

____

____

____

____

____

Upon finishing the SWOT analysis, you should have a better assessment of where you currently are within your career path, how to stand out and where development might be needed. All these factors can then be utilized to find favorable growth opportunities along your career path.

Starting with "Why"

Where do you see yourself in 5, 10, 20 or 30 years? Everyone comes across this question at least once in a lifetime and generally everyone wants a career destination that bears a resemblance to a true calling and not just a job. In order to get to that level of satisfaction, starting with "why" is crucial. Your "why" gives you a sense of purpose, a desire for existence, a clear view of the impact you are aiming for along your professional journey. Accomplishing your "why" is success in the purest form. However, defining success as accomplishing your "why" is often uncommon among professionals.

Throughout my career so far, I have met more individuals who are frustrated about their careers relative to those that truly derive satisfaction from it. It almost always boils down to three things. The individual is trapped within the desire for a higher job title, compensation or unsure of the chosen career path. Most professionals are not where they hope to be on the success spectrum. For some, it is no fault of theirs, people attain success at different stages in life and success is only a matter of time. For most, the problem usually stems from their definition of success.

Success is usually centered on materialistic aspirations or a desire to impress. For the materialistic aspirants, true success is the friend that drives the latest model of their dream car, the family member with a bank account that is big enough to sponsor generations to Ivy League colleges, and the manager at work that owns a private jet. For those with a desire to impress, their original career goals usually get sidetracked as the need to impress their peers supersedes the career path they would have truly enjoyed.

A reassessed definition of success, which starts with truly knowing your "why", is the best route to a purposeful career that unveils your true calling. There will be many tough choices to make along a career path. When your "why" is clear, it is easier to make choices that will increase the chances of making it through the road bumps along the way.

I found my "why" during a summer vacation to Nigeria in 2010. During the trip, I had a severe allergic reaction and almost lost my life due to an erratic supply of electricity at the time. I had difficulty breathing and my parents rushed me to the nearest private hospital with the hope of it being equipped with the necessary infrastructure. Unfortunately, we arrived at the hospital during a power outage and the generator, which was supposed to supply back-up power to the hospital, was not functional.

After I had my son during the coronavirus pandemic, my mind travelled back a decade to the traumatic experience. With the onset of COVID-19, concerns such as possible separation from my family and the fear of being an asymptomatic carrier got added to the list of worries. If I were in a developing country, basic human need such as electricity might have been added to the list. Giving birth is a beautiful yet difficult process. No one should have to worry about the lack of electricity as an additional layer of complexity within the process.

As of 2019, approximately 1 billion people across the globe lacked access to consistent electricity. After the 2010 ordeal, I often ponder why electricity was such a scarce and inaccessible resource in one of the top oil producing countries. This built the foundation for my drive and passion for enabling better standard of living by finding innovative ways to bridge the gap between resource availability and accessibility; which summaries my "why". If you take nothing else away from this book, I hope it encourages you to find a reason to make an impact in something so strong that you ponder about it during the day and dream about it while asleep.

When we start out as professionals, the first impulse is to survive; pay the student loans, build a life where we do the things we love and get settled. The financial reward of our profession allows us to live the lives we want. That is baseline. Your "why" allows you to tap into a purpose-centric career that goes far beyond the baseline.

A helpful way to tap into your why is to evaluate the things you do for free that bring you a sense of fulfillment and joy and find a way to align those things with your career strengths and opportunities. In my case, I love to volunteer for charitable and educational causes. My earliest volunteer activity I can recollect was at the tender age of 12. Over the years I have held official positions with different nonprofit organizations with the ultimate goal of positively impacting as many lives as possible. I will gladly dedicate time, effort and resources to a cause I believe in. In the same light, a devotion to enabling better standard of living by finding innovative ways to bridge the gap between resource availability and accessibility excites me as anybody's "why" should. A good test for knowing that you have successfully unveiled your “why” within your professional life is to evaluate if you are equally excited while at work, compared to while doing the things you love without getting paid.

The Destination

After unveiling your "why", to determine where you want to take your career to, imagine you are at your retirement party, being celebrated for an impactful career that accomplished your "why". As people take turns at the podium to honor your years of service, envision what you would like them to say about you. Imagine what your favorite statements will be for the evening, statements regarding your character, values and accomplishments, centered around your "why". Then write down the statements below.

Character Statements at Retirement

____

____

____

____

____

____

Value Statements at Retirement

____

____

____

____

____

____

"Why" centered Accomplishment Statements at Retirement

____
____
____
____
____
____

Essentially, the statements above serve as a note to the future. In order to become the person within these statements, find someone that is presently at the destination you want to aim for based on your statements above. It might be possible to find one person that meets all specifications within the statements above, but multiple individuals will work also. A good source for this exercise is LinkedIn. Go through profiles to identify experts within your industry of interest.

The key takeaway is to identify an individual, study the trajectory taken by the individual in order to get to the current state of their career. Study the individual's positions, trainings and educational development over their career. Also, what did the individual do to go above and beyond their basic job; did they volunteer within their community, publish in journals or were they known as a key value-adding leader. This will give you a rough draft of the roadmap for your career journey. You are not aiming to follow the person's footsteps exactly, but it helps to give a sense of direction that can be fine-tuned as you build your career. When you start with a road map, arriving at your destination is easier and far more efficient because you have a better understanding of the opportunities to go after in order to stay on course.

Goal-Setting

Upon attaining a clear understanding of the current state of your career, the "why" behind your professional journey and the destination, the next step toward a purposeful career is setting and achieving career goals that lead to the destination. When well-thought-out career goals are laid out, it provides actionable milestones that serve as confirmation that progress is being made toward achieving your full career potential. You do not have to worry about ever feeling like you are not getting anywhere because there is proof that you are, as each milestone gets crossed off the list.

An effective way to set career goals is to work backwards. This allows the ability to focus on the end goal while breaking long-term goals into smaller short-term goals with career objectives that act as stepping-stones to your career progression. These set goals must be written down and SMART; Specific, Measurable, Attainable, Relevant and Time Based.

Writing down your goals is important for the successful attainment of the goals as numerous studies have shown that people have better memory of things written down. If you cannot clearly remember your goals, success is far-fetched. When writing down your goals, make them as clear as possible, include drawings and pictures if necessary and ultimately make it easily comprehendible to the extent that a stranger will know exactly what you aim to achieve.

SMART goals come into play as a technique for increasing a goal's success rate. The acronym SMART stands for Specific, Measurable, Attainable, Relevant and Time Based. SMART goals therefore incorporate these five elements to help increase clarity and chances of achieving your goals. Think back to the roadmap from the last chapter. Based on your destination, evaluate what your long-term and short-term goals are and write them down as SMART goals starting on the next page. They can be as little as 3 and as much as 10 or more. The aim is to have them align with your "why", character, values and targeted future accomplishments. Also, your goals should align with the organization or avenue through which you aim to fulfill the career goals by making sure your career goals add value to the organization's overarching goal.

Specific

What is the exact goal?

Goal 1:

Goal 2:

Goal 3:

Goal 4:

Goal 5:

Goal 6:

Goal 7:

Goal 8:

Goal 9:

Goal 10:

Measurable

What are the metrics that will be used to measure progress and success of the goal?

Goal 1:

Goal 2:

Goal 3:

Goal 4:

Goal 5:

Goal 6:

Goal 7:

Goal 8:

Goal 9:

Goal 10:

Attainable

What are the necessary skillsets needed to achieve the goal? If skillsets are not readily available, how will they be obtained?

Goal 1:

Goal 2:

Goal 3:

Goal 4:

Goal 5:

Goal 6:

Goal 7:

Goal 8:

Goal 9:

Goal 10:

Relevant

Thinking back to your "why" is the goal beneficial in the grand scheme of a fulfilling career?

Goal 1:

Goal 2:

Goal 3:

Goal 4:

Goal 5:

Goal 6:

Goal 7:

Goal 8:

Goal 9:

Goal 10:

Time Based

When will you start working toward the goal and when do you aim to accomplish the goal?

Goal 1:

Goal 2:

Goal 3:

Goal 4:

Goal 5:

Goal 6:

Goal 7:

Goal 8:

Goal 9:

Goal 10:

Win & Mentorship

When goals are set, it is often forgotten that strategies are needed in order to achieve the set goals. Goals are essentially targeted outcomes we hope to accomplish, while strategy focuses on the necessary actions that help achieve the targeted outcomes. Win and Mentorship are the two words that I take into consideration when setting a goal achievement strategy. The strategy should start with an evaluation of the best way to win. For example, assuming you are a young professional with a career goal of learning a new technical skill. Within the evaluation of how to win are the options of volunteering to take on a technical project that provides exposure to the technical skill of interest, enrolling in a technical training course or reading a recommended technical book. Basically, with your current capability, explore the most effective options that have the potential of leading to a win.

While win serves as potential doors that lead to goal achievement strategies, mentorship holds the key to the doors. Throughout my career path, I have come to realize that mentorship is the most important element for developing strategies for career goals. Isaac Newton sums it up quite nicely. "If I have seen further than others, it is by standing on the shoulders of giants". Giants are the individuals with years of experience ahead of us that can help strengthen individual efforts and empower us with the support and knowledge needed to make better decisions. Continuing with the example of a young professional with a career goal of learning a new technical skill, identifying a person who has already acquired the technical skill of interest and learning about the route the Mentor took, what worked, what did not and what could have been done better is very important. Equally important is leading with intent instead of questions.

I have learned to get the best out of mentorship by leading with intent instead of questions. Often, we set short-term goals thinking they are the link to a long-term goal, sometimes they are, sometimes they are not. From our earlier example, assuming that learning a new technical skill is a short-term goal that is believed to be linked to a long-term goal of succeeding at a new role, the conversation should be led with "I intend to succeed at this role by learning a new technical skill". This way, the Mentor can ascertain if obtaining a new technical skill is the most effective strategy for achieving the long-term goal of succeeding at the role of interest.

Apart from strategy development for career goals, working alongside Mentors makes it possible to ease the pain, see hope in your vision and increase the chances of success when the journey inevitably gets hard. Careers are meant to be challenging in order to grow, so embrace the challenging times when they come alongside trusted advisors. No matter what industry or company you work for, a sure way to succeed is to add effective value in the process of meeting your career goals. Evaluate skills that are unique to your industry and add effective value through those that resonate with you. My personal favorite is innovation and its application to filling in organizational gaps in order to enable continuous progress toward a better standard of living for the society. Upon narrowing down the skills you want to master, find Mentors that emulate each skill. Throughout our lives, Mentors such as family, friends, teachers and many other role models have been instrumental in shaping us into who we are today. We are the average of the people we associate with. Therefore, finding and keeping good Mentors that emulate the skills you hope to master will enhance those skills within you.

Some Mentors will be instrumental in helping you fine-tune your strategy for meeting your career goals, others will be instrumental in specific skills, others will function more as a life coach, the bottom-line is that it is almost impossible to live out a purposeful career without the help of Mentors. The process of acquiring Mentors should be started with a wide net for potential Mentors. It can be a quick or long process but take enough time to learn about your potential Mentors and how they can be of help before requesting to be mentored. Sometimes, the fear of rejection sets in; how can a well-accomplished person have the time and energy to help a novice like me? Remember every single expert was once a novice. As long as you ask respectfully, the worst answer you can get is a "No", which takes nothing away from you. As a matter of fact, get used to "No", the average successful person says it a lot. Warren Buffett often credits his success to saying no. One of my favorite quotes from him says, "the difference between successful people and really successful people is that really successful people say no to almost everything". Ever wonder why you cannot seem to get enough time in 24 hours and yet CEOs and Presidents manage corporations and countries in the same daily time allotment, the secret is in time management. A lot of "No" is needed to allow enough time for the crucial things that need "Yes". You want a

Mentor that genuinely believes your success is worth their time and those Mentors are out there, you just have to find the right ones. When you do find the right ones, assure that all commitments can be honored, as it is important to respect a Mentor's time and effort. In the long run, seek out Mentors who can become sponsors with the main difference being someone who is willing to transition from giving advice and support to someone who is actively advocating for your career progression. Below are 4 steps to help you find good Mentors.

1. Find potential Mentors who have experience that aligns with your career goals and skills or attributes that you want to emulate.
2. Request a meeting with each potential Mentor to discuss the level of guidance you are seeking, what purpose the guidance will serve and the amount of time commitment you are seeking.
3. After the meeting, spend some time reflecting on the meeting discussion and evaluate how you feel after the initial communication with the individual.
    - Do you feel encouraged and motivated to do better?

- Is this a person you can see yourself learning more from?
- Do you sense the willingness to share knowledge and expertise?
- Is the individual respectful and able to give and receive honest feedback?

4. If the answers to the questions above are yes, you can proceed to asking the individual to be your Mentor. If any of the answers to the questions above is no, I would advise you to go back to step 1 and find new potential Mentors.

At the end of this book is a 52 weeks mentorship journal to guide and encourage weekly meetings with Mentors. As with anything in life, change is inevitable along a career path. As the world continues to change and evolve, industries will be impacted which might require adjustments to your career goals. The journal is meant to help encourage a culture of mentorship, track your career goals progress and make any necessary adjustments to your goals and strategies for achieving them.

Seizing Opportunities

If you have a clear understanding of the current state of your career, your "why", your career destination, your goals and strategies for achieving them while keying into the power of mentorship, you are halfway prepared for a purposeful career. The other half is imbedded in the act of seizing opportunities. Rarely are things handed over in life but unfortunately, it is easier to seek permission than it is to take initiative. It is easier to wait for a new assignment at work than it is to create a project that increases the company's growth objectives.

Our natural instinct is to wait to get picked. However, when seeking to maximize your career goals in order to awaken a fulfilling career that makes a long-lasting difference, you cannot wait to be selected. No one will ever understand the burning desire behind your "why" as much as you do, so no one will fight for it to become reality as much as you can. You must learn to seize opportunities by being an avid learner with a strong work ethic and devotion to finding, solving and vocalizing problems.

From a half full cup perspective, problems can be opportunities for growth and improvement. Think for a minute about technological advancements over the years. Try to recall an obsolete gadget such as the typewriter that has been replaced with a compact, time saving, user-friendly, alternative such a computer. Think about the technological advancement in education. Through online learning, geographical barriers to quality education can be further broken down. In essence, there will always be problems to solve for the betterment of humanity.

Problems however are often unnoticed or dwelled on till they become productivity inhibitors. It is imperative to learn to identify problems, so as to not miss the opportunities they might present. One effective way of identifying problems is to make a detailed list of factors and questions hindering the transition from a current situation to a desired situation. When you identify a problem, be sure to understand the value proposition involved in solving the problem. This ascertains that the opportunity, if present, is valuable to the organization when capitalized upon. When you discover a value adding opportunity, aim to make it a habit to show initiative by providing input to potential solutions. Potential solutions do not have to be perfect; the more important aspect is to make sure potential solutions are vocalized, so let your voice be heard. The power to make a positive change in an organization lies within a balanced objective voice. Often times when you share a potential solution to a problem, your suggestion either leads to a breakthrough or spark an idea in someone else, which then leads to a breakthrough. Either way, a voiced potential solution is one step closer to a breakthrough. This stands you out as an individual who is aligned with continuous value creation for an organization. Only when there is continuous value creation that aligns with your "why" can there be opportunity to step out of your comfort zone and into a purpose-centric career.

Opportunity Stories

These are stories of those currently seeking the next opportunity. Even if you do not have an opportunity to offer, let these stories encourage you to search for and share a job opportunity with someone in need. The email address of each individual is included to allow readers to pass on any advice or opportunities.

Akshay Dehadray

akshdehadray@gmail.com

Westcliff University: PhD, Business Administration and Management 2023

Westcliff University: MBA, Business Statistics and Data Analytics 2020

I am originally from Mumbai India and recently graduated with an MBA in Business Statistics and Data Analytics. Prior to that, I bagged two Master's degrees in Computer Information Systems and Biomedical Engineering. Currently, I am pursuing my Doctor of Business Administration in Business Intelligence, Data Analytics and IT Management. I am very passionate about Project Management, Business Intelligence and foresee myself having a career leading to a Senior Project Manager and eventually an executive level position after receiving my Doctorate.

I have mainly been working as a Business Analyst so far. Being an international student, I have made utmost effort to the best of my ability on my end to gain relative professional experience while pursuing my education. My contract job ended a few months ago. Even though Covid-19 didn't result in the termination of my contract, the pandemic has definitely slowed the overall hiring process, making it challenging to find a relevant position. Until I find an opportunity, I am making efforts to learn new skill sets and obtain certifications, which can highlight my profile and help me in securing the next role.

Amir Rastboud

marastboud@gmail.com

Texas A&M University: MS Data Analytics 2022

University of Houston: BS Petroleum Engineering 2019

I obtained a bachelor's degree in Foreign Language and Translation from Azad University in Iran. After graduation, I worked as an ESL (English as a Second Language) instructor in Iran for almost five years. Because of my admiration for American technology and opportunities, I came to the USA alone without any financial support to pursue my dreams. In the beginning, life was difficult, and I had to work from the bottom all the way up in variety of jobs including hotels, restaurants, and retails. Along the way, I always held the belief that I could do so much more with my problem solving and analytical thinking skills.

Eventually, I decided to work towards a different academic path and study Petroleum Engineering. It's been always fascinating to me how technology advanced in the oil and gas industry since centuries ago in order to get crude oil from thousands of feet under the ground and bring it to the surface in the most economic, effective, and safe way. Not to mention, it was extremely challenging to study engineering without a background in engineering. So, I had to learn Math and Physics from the very beginning and worked much harder than most of my classmates.

As a college student, I was lucky enough to obtain a Petroleum Engineering Internship with Aramco, during which I conducted research on produced-water treatments processes for oil and gas wells. My other internship was with Precision Well Logging. As a mud logger, I had the opportunity to get my hands dirty and learn about drilling operations and analyzing rock samples to determine formation lithology. In addition, during this period, I served as an active board member of Society of Petroleum Engineers (SPE)-University of Houston Student Chapter.

I overcame many academic obstacles and graduated with Magna Cum Laude in Petroleum Engineering from the University of Houston. After graduation, I have been struggling with securing a position due to COVID-19 and the oil market crisis but I am not letting this setback destroy my dream. I refuse to give up because I have come this far! Of course, there are days with self-doubt and hopelessness. However, with my determination, I managed to turn desperation into inspiration. Knowing that multidisciplinary engineering is the future, I decided to expand the horizon and enrolled in the Master of Data Analytics program in Texas A&M University where I am actively learning programming and robotics.

I honestly have no idea how the future is going to turn out given the current circumstances, yet I truly believe that the key to stay hopeful is to keep working and improving upon your dreams. I did not come all the way to America to give up on my engineering dreams! I would be happy to share my experience in more detail if interested.

Anshum Jain

anshum.jain@tamu.edu

Texas A&M University: Master's degree, Mechanical Engineering 2021

Manipal Institute of Technology: Bachelors, Mechanical Engineering 2019

As an international student, internship search is already difficult enough. I interviewed with a company but received no response. Most of the positions I applied to were cancelled. I was dependent on the stipend from the internship to make rent and since I do not have an internship, that aspect of my life has become a tad bit tougher. As a mechanical engineer in the COVID world, majority of the work cannot be done from home and employers avoid hiring recent grads as training is not possible while working from home and the new hires are not familiar with the work culture of the company.

I will appreciate any form of help that can be rendered. I am currently enrolled at Texas A&M University, pursuing a master's degree in mechanical engineering. I will be graduating in May 2021. I am open to any job opportunities in the areas of mechanical design and manufacturing. Getting a Spring 2021 co-op and a full time position upon graduation in 2021 is my immediate goal. I have had some internship experience and have ample experience using CAD software

(AutoCAD, Solidworks, Fusion 360) and simulation software (ANSYS-Beginner).

Avirat Kshar

avirat.kshar@mavs.uta.edu

The University of Texas at Arlington: MS, Industrial Engineering 2020

Veermata Jijabai Technological Institute: Bachelor of Technology, Mechanical Engineering 2018

I received a Diploma in Mechanical Engineering from a reputable institute in India. However, I saw hurdles in my way to pursue higher education and took a break for months. I finally realized I was missing the way to great achievements and paved my way to the United States pursuing master's in industrial engineering from the University of Texas at Arlington.

After a few months of applications, interviews and rejections, I finally landed an internship with Volvo Group as a Logistics Engineer. My Dream came TRUE... but so did Covid-19. The next thing I saw was an email stating the offer had been rescinded. Everything came to a pause but not my dreams. COVID-19 has not only affected substantial growth of learning curve but also morally declined the vision to achieve it. The situation has caused downfall in number of job postings, increase in number of layoffs and thus struggles to look for jobs.

I am looking for opportunities in the field of supply chain, logistics and continuous improvement. I have also done extensive research in areas of automation, thermodynamics, automobile and green manufacturing along with professional experience in manufacturing industry for about 2 years. I am currently working as a research assistant at UTA on the project; energy cost analysis in 3D printing. I am looking for vivid learning, ability to grow professionally along with challenges in industrial background and practical exposure. All I need is a chance to make a difference.

Deborah Mepaiyeda

dmepaiyeda@gmail.com

Ryerson University: BS Computer Science 2020

I am a final year student at Ryerson University studying Computer Science. After a year of hard work and improving my skills, I secured a Software Engineering internship with a well-known retail company for a Software Engineering internship starting in June 2020. However, my offer was rescinded due to COVID-19 and I was very disappointed.

After reflecting on my situation, I decided to focus on the positive. I began doing additional learning to improve my technical skills. I also thought that the best thing to do is to continue to improve myself and apply for full-time roles. I have occupied five positions in various companies. My first role was in an e-commerce startup where I worked as a Front-End Web Developer to build an online marketplace for hotel room service. In my next position, I was an Innovation Engineer for Scotiabank's Capital Market. I worked with five developers to build a web application that streamlines data for the company's employees—this increased employee productivity by 20%. In my next two placements, I worked as a Developer and Full-Stack Developer for RBC's Digital team and Capital Markets Department, respectively. As a Full-Stack, I created visualization features and wrote tests for the company's Investment Advisor web app— this improved the app by 30%. As a Developer for the Digital team, I created special features to improve the banking experience for customers and wrote various tests to improve the banking platform.

Also, I led and participated in Agile activities such as stand-up, backlog refinement meetings and sprint planning. In one of the sprints, I was a Scrum Master, where I worked closely with the Product Owner of the project and led a team of ten to develop and push code to production. My most recent role was as a Software Developer at Rangle.io. I worked on two projects – an email signature web application and improved a web app for a major retailer. I upgraded the signature app for 300 employees and migrated it from Google Cloud Platform to AWS. In the second project, I enhanced different features in the retailer's app, improving the user experience and usability.

In all these roles, I worked on teams of varying sizes and collaborated with designers, developers and stakeholders. These experiences have greatly enhanced my skills as a developer, and I am sharpening my skills even more during this time. I will be grateful if anyone can be of assistance in any way. I'm interested in Software Development, Front-End Development and UX Development. Industries such as e-commerce, health and wellness, travel, retail, and food interest me. I am also open to various tech industries. Thank you for taking the time to read this.

Eric Azodeh

eazodeh@tamu.edu

Texas A&M University: BS, Computer Science 2022

Hello, my name is Eric Azodeh. I am a junior at Texas A&M University pursuing a Bachelor of Science in Computer Science. My interest in the energy industry was revealed early on into my sophomore year of college when I took a visit to the ExxonMobil campus in Spring, Texas and met with several other energy companies at our school's career fair. I enjoyed the distinct tasks each energy company displayed to me. Whether it was handling large amounts of data and using my programming skills to analyze trends and behavior, or it was implementing software to deter the growing threat of cyber-terrorism, the numerous roles that the energy companies described appealed to me greatly.

After some tough decisions, I eventually accepted an Information Technology internship offer with Occidental Petroleum for the summer of 2020. After deciding to intern with Oxy in the incoming summer, that same summer that initially was empty and without plans became packed with a 40 hour/week, full-time internship. Unfortunately, about 3 weeks before the start date, I received the call that my offer was rescinded due to everything going on regarding Covid-19 and the plummet of oil prices. I was disappointed because I was extremely excited to start my first internship, and it would have filled my summer schedule up in a meaningful way. However, I had to face reality and look at the bright side of the situation. I had to look ahead and not dwell on what was, *but what is*.

I thought about my once-filled summer 2020 that is now vacant, ready to be filled. Of course, I can fill up that empty space with idle activities like waking up late every day and binge-watching as many TV shows as possible, but I decided to fill it up with worthwhile, meaningful activities. Without an internship, it's now time for me to step up and become my own boss, manager, and mentor. Any goals set to be completed over this summer would be made *by me* and expected to be completed *by me*. I made sure to reach out to Oxy to determine which skills I would have been working on. With their feedback, I immediately began fine-tuning my skills in C/C++, as well as learning new programming languages such as SQL and JavaScript. I added 9 extra hours to my summer course load to remain busy over the break, and I made sure to pick up a new interest, stock trading, which helps me with discipline in waking up early in the morning at 7:30 am to start my day off and get to work. I also used this vacant time to spend more time with friends and family, being able to encourage and motivate them as they are going through similar situations as me.

The way that I looked at the whole situation was that different companies offered me an internship because they saw potential in me. Even without an internship, I have to make sure that I'm using that same potential they saw in me to develop myself over this peculiar summer. An internship cancellation is *not* the end of the world. You have got to adapt to the situation at hand and work on yourself over that vacant period of time; you will be surprised at how much you can accomplish by yourself while preparing for the next big opportunity.

Fitore Balidemaj

fitorebali@gmail.com

Eastern Connecticut State University: Bachelors, Management Information Systems and Services 2020

The class of 2020 will notoriously be looked back on as the one who lucked out: no real graduation, no real goodbye to their undergraduate life, and no real identity outside of being the graduating class during a global pandemic. I find it difficult to talk about how COVID-19 impacted my job search, when these last few months have affected my life all around. It took years of advocating for myself to convince my immigrant parents to let me move to New York City if I got a job or internship offer after graduation. After all that perseverance & hard work, it was taken away in the blink of an eye as we entered a global pandemic.

Although I didn't get to have the actual intern experience that I accepted, I'm currently planning to complete a virtual internship unique to my interests this summer with Eastern Connecticut State University (ECSU) Business Information Systems department. Once I receive those credits, I will be able to begin my professional career. At the moment, I'm trying to figure out how to juggle my responsibilities while taking care of my mom, who successfully battled cancer during this pandemic. It's difficult to experience all these emotions at once when people are dying at alarming rates and my problems feel incredibly minimized in retrospect. Nonetheless, one of my greatest qualities is that I am determined. In my 21 years, I've found that determination is the key to success because it enables us to persist in the face of difficulties. This side of my personality came in handy in my college courses as I became more adept in problem solving. Prior to the virus outbreak in March, I was volunteering for a local STEM middle school in a technology program called "Puentes al Futuro" (Bridges to the Future). I looked forward to it every week, sometimes because I felt like I learned more from them than they did from me.

Our main goal as mentors was to instill effective learning tactics through each activity and emphasize the importance of team contribution. Common lessons included how to build a robot out of different types of materials, and then applying coding to make the robots function. It was intriguing to watch young minds accomplish tasks that I know some college professors aren't even capable of. In such a short time, the other volunteers & I built an amazing bond with the students.

Watching how they work their way through a problem made me change how I see challenges, and for that I am forever grateful. Aside from volunteering this school year, I worked part time as an assistant at an ECSU residential hall and at a local car dealership.

Although both jobs had entirely different agendas, they both helped me strengthen my technical and communication skills and apply my studies to real time work. There are so many different careers paths I could take with my degree and my diverse skill set. At the moment, I am most interested in finding a position in Project Management and/or Business Intelligence. With the help of my professors and challenging coursework throughout the last 4 years, I'm confident that I can get it done. It is also important to me that I work for a company whose values align with mine. Jobs are like little communities within themselves. There are so many movements that need support right now and I want to be a part of a community that is actively trying to make a change in the world.

Honson Tran

honsontran@gmail.com

Rutgers University-New Brunswick: BS, Computer Science 2020

I am a recent graduate of Rutgers University with a bachelor's degree in computer science. With everything going on in 2020, I've unfortunately lost my grandmother, lived through my first school lockdown, and also gotten my full time offer as a machine-learning engineer frozen due to coronavirus. However, I'm still trying my hardest each day to continue to learn and grow for the next big opportunity.

My interests and future career goals lie in artificial intelligence and computer vision. I believe the thought of making computers learn how to "see" is one of the most important things humanity is working on in conjunction with AI. For my ultimate goal, I want to continue to gain enough knowledge to participate in the global discussion on how AI will be regulated and used for good. Essentially, I strongly feel that being an awesome thought leader in the space is my way of impacting the world.

Currently, my career and short-term goal is to secure a full time offer in the Bay Area. I was born in San Francisco, but never got a chance to live there. I moved at a couple months old after an unfortunate gun robbery at our home. My mom's side of the family is all the way back on the West coast, and it would be a dream to finally return home. Along with this goal, I've been working hard to get publications and continue doing research in hopes of being accepted to Stanford for a PhD program.

Kevin Huynh, EIT

kiemvinh1998@gmail.com

St. Mary's University: BS Mechanical Engineering 2020

I was ready, excited to begin my college journey back in 2016. I thought to myself I could finally become a mechanical engineer in 2020. I love solving problems and being a part of the team that can make an impact in the society. I started with teaching robotics, tutoring programming, researching flexible batteries, and joining organizations. Each experience helped me understand my limitation and widen my horizon. I was blessed to be trusted and given opportunities to take on organizational responsibilities (IEEE and ASME Petroleum Division Collegiate Council). After completing 2 internships, I was confident and ready to realize my dream of being an Engineer. I took my Fundamentals of Engineering (FE) exam so that I could take my Professional Engineer (PE) exam after graduation. I devote myself to being a licensed Professional Engineer. My Mentor, Sean Berg, inspires and shows me how to be an engineer and a team player.

Then COVID-19 hit everyone. I was worried for my family, my Professors who are the most vulnerable and the exhausted health care providers on the front lines. I have friends who are Nurses and Physicians, so I could feel their burnout. I wanted to use my engineering skills to render help, so I designed and 3D printed ear savers for my local nurses and friends to prevent headaches, chafing, and even blisters. As of now, I have printed over 500 ear savers, donated to medical professionals, friends, and families. Unfortunately, I had to stop because I ran out of filaments and the supply became scarce. I want to use my engineering skills to contribute to society. I would love to continue making CAD designs, improving efficiency, and working with other Engineers to deliver the best solution for a client. I have worked in a startup environment and I would like to transcend the entrepreneurial spirit along with my team. I am looking for a Mechanical Engineer position where I can work well in a small team.

Kuan Chen

kuanhc96@uchicago.edu

University of Chicago: Master's, Computer Science 2020

University of Washington: BS, Computational and Applied Mathematics, Chemical Engineering 2019

I came to the US 7 years ago from Taiwan as an international student for high school. At the time, I did not know where my journey was headed, but I was full of excitement, hoping to one day live the American Dream. In my high school years, I received overwhelming support and kindness from friends, family and my church community when applying to college. I was ecstatic when I was accepted to the University of Washington (UW), and quickly decided to pursue a career in Chemical Engineering, thinking that this, surely, would get me closer to realizing my dreams.

However, in my Junior year, as I started applying for internships, I was met with the harsh reality that, many engineering industries put strict limitations on hiring international students for work. This is most evident in the aviation industry, where many companies have contracts with the government, and the chemicals industry, where many companies have proprietary secrets. For these reasons, as an international student with a background in chemical engineering, with little connections in the US, I realized that my chances for employment were grim.

Despite various setbacks, I continued to receive support and encouragement from my friends and family. I was advised to be patient, keep applying, but also actively seek out new opportunities. UW, being in the heart of Seattle, was known for its role in fueling the tech industry in the area. For the fun of it, I decided to take advantage of the school's resources in computer science, and took classes offered by the department just to try my hands on it. My initial intrigue in the industry led me to pursuing a second degree at the UW, in applied mathematics. Once again, I was hopeful that my talents would eventually get a chance to shine, as long as I am willing to put the work into it.

I graduated from the UW in the summer of 2019, with a double degree in chemical engineering and applied math. Now, equipped with extensive experience in math and programming, I decided that I could now give it a shot at pursuing a degree in computer science. Luckily, I received an offer from my top-choice school, the University of Chicago, to further my education. With a renewed confidence in my capabilities, as soon as I moved to Chicago in fall of 2019, I started applying for summer internships. In the fall quarter alone, I applied for around 150 positions all over the country, primarily focusing on places where I had networking connections. Through my connections, I was able to get referrals, and later interviews, relatively easy. However, I lacked the technical interviewing experience that many of my peers had. Nonetheless, I continued refining my resume, applied to more jobs, attended mock interviews, and finally towards the end of February, I was given an offer for Java development internship in the heart of downtown Chicago. Extremely satisfied with the offer and benefits that the company provided, I quickly signed my contract with them, securing a position with the company. This happened only one week prior to Illinois statewide lockdown.

Throughout the spring quarter, I observed a spate of people being laid-off from their jobs, job offers rescinded, and internships canceled. This happened to many of my most qualified friends in Seattle, and I started to feel apprehensive about my future prospects again. The fact is, without an internship, not only would finding full-time jobs become a lot harder in the future, I would not even be able to graduate from my program with the specialization I wanted because the University of Chicago's MSCS program requires students who want to graduate with a specialization to complete an internship related to that specialization. Thus, despite having accepted an internship offer, I decided to keep applying, just in case something unexpected were to happen.

To my surprise, in April, the recruiter I interviewed with reached out to me informing me that the company will definitely be following through with their internship program, and that I need not worry about my summer plans. I felt relieved, thinking that, despite the disheartening lockdown crisis, there were still things I could look forward to after all. I stopped applying to other internships, thinking that I had nothing to worry about.

Unfortunately, the same recruiter who interviewed me, who gave me an offer, and who reassured me that the internship would continue, called me back to inform me that the company decided to cancel their internship program. My heart sunk, knowing that my chances to find an internship in late May 2020 were never grimmer, as most companies who still had internships already commenced their programs, Looking through job boards, unsurprisingly, there were little to no open positions for hiring interns.

Without any work experience in tech, and unable to complete my specialization program, I am expected to graduate into an economy that has been at its worst since the great depression. Mounted with student debt, accumulated from my undergraduate years and now into grad school, it feels as though my goal toward the American Dream is as far as ever. Hopefully, as the country reopens, new opportunities will be available, and the economy will recover quickly. As of now, I continue to seek ways to better myself, and look forward to finding new opportunities to help me achieve my goals.

Linda Huang

lindathehuang@gmail.com

University of California, Davis: Bachelor of Arts, Design 2019

My name is Linda Huang, I'm a web and graphic designer. I graduated from the University of California, Davis last December. I have a bachelor's degree in Design, with minors in Psychology and Communication, and I am currently finishing a certification in Web Design as part of the continuing professional education at my University. I'm a published children's book illustrator for the children's novel, Kingdom of the Silver Cat. I'm interested in projects that focus on social good and I am especially passionate about sustainability and mental health.

In 2017, during my second year in the University, I became fascinated with coding for design. I was introduced to the Processing Programming language and worked on the large-scale interactive projection portion of a sustainable lounge space installation, called BLOOM. We designed this 97% sustainable lounge space using cardboard and biomaterials for furniture. These included scoby from kombucha, mycelium (the branching reproductive parts of mushrooms) mixed with wood waste, and organic wool. I coded a generative 30ft tall projection using Processing, and presented the combined installation in Chicago with my team as one of only 6 selected nation-wide schools at the SOFA Connect conference for Sculptural Art and Design. This project greatly influenced my fascination towards biodesign, biomimicry, and designing for sustainability. This was also around the time that I started taking classes for and became interested in web design.

In my last year at Davis in early 2019, I was on boarded as a graphics lead by a hardware acceleration organization called Hard Tech Fund, which started as a club on campus. At Hard Tech Fund, I completely designed the visual identity, created social media marketing materials, and developed and coded the website. In summer of 2019, we assisted multiple sustainable hardware projects that were presented at our Demo Day in San Francisco, attended by investors. We have since evolved into a non-profit and are planning to assist the development of multiple hyperloop transportation projects across the country.

During my last year, I also worked as a web designer and content manager at the campus's Energy and Efficiency Department's D-Lab. D-Lab assists countries and organizations abroad in need of assistance, provides solutions to community issues and infrastructure, and helps set up environmentally-aware education systems focusing on zero-waste and zero-net energy. I completely redesigned their website from Wordpress to the campus's content management system, Sitefarm. I was invigorated with knowing that I professionalized the D-Lab website, created a better communication platform for those in need abroad, and structured the site in a way that was understandable and easy to navigate for my successor.

While on lockdown, after multiple final-stage interviews with no call-backs, and months of more job-hunting, I started getting more proactive with the time I would have spent job-hunting. I dove into project after project. First, it was a revamp of my portfolio, which I'd re-coded for the fifth time. I also started freelancing during this time, which is something I'd never thought I'd do. I created static websites for clients and provided heuristic feedback for their projects. Then I (along with three others) developed a 24-hour hackathon project called LinkedUp, which helps job seekers keep track of their LinkedIn connections with message templates. My team and I shared our project and experiences on the career platform, Wonsulting, to hundreds of viewers.

After that I dove into a week-long hacking sprint project called Clove, in which we designed a website and user experience system for food delivery to seniors (which we won the award for most original solution). I've also been onboarded as a designer for SacHacks, a 24-hour Sacramento Hackathon I've participated in (and won awards for) twice. All were projects and involvements that I appreciated, but they didn't quite satiate my itch for working with environmental awareness.

Then a friend I made at a SacHacks two years ago in 2018 messaged me after seeing my projects. He said he thought of a project. One that will help people be more ethical in their shopping habits. A Chrome extension that rates businesses on how ethical they are, in terms of sustainable practices, labor practices, etc. I'm looking forward to developing this project and more projects like this that make me feel like I'm doing something good.

Nicholas Hughes

hugh8747@stthomas.edu

University of St. Thomas: Bachelor's Degree, Financial Management 2020

I am a recent graduate from the University of St. Thomas in Saint Paul, Minnesota. I graduated with Latin honors, with a major in Finance and a minor in Theology. After two successful internships one at a small local company and the other at a medical device company, Boston Scientific, I went into the Fall of my senior year, excited to apply and interview for all the different opportunities coming to campus for our season of on-campus interviews. Following several interviews and offers, I decided to take a job at a local consulting firm working in valuation of middle market companies for purposes of ESOPs (Employee Stock Ownership Plans) as well as mergers and acquisitions work. I was ecstatic. The company was full of a lot alumni, I got along extremely well with everyone I talked to, the company had a great culture with a huge emphasis on ethics, and most importantly it seemed like a place I could go in and work hard and learn a ton. After this, I was ready to enjoy my senior year and take in many great memories the year had to offer. Unfortunately, COVID-19 happened. I thought I was safe for a while but as things got worse, I got an email in late April informing me that my offer was rescinded. This was hard news to take, I felt like I did everything right. I worked hard to get two internships so when an opportunity came around like this, I would be qualified. I worked hard to receive my offer back in October 2019 so I could enjoy my senior year.

During my internship with Boston Scientific, I worked in a department called Global Business Services. This group served as a back-office support for offices and plants all over the world. I worked with co-workers in Ireland, India, and across the United States to improve accounting processes as well as helping with month end activities. At the end of the summer, I got to visit the headquarters in Boston and present my projects to senior management. My previous internship was at a company called Energy Management Collaborative, which dealt with lighting retrofitting and energy efficiency. I worked mostly in the Accounts Payable department processing payments but had different projects in Tax and Audits.

I chose Finance as a major because it is the backbone of business and has endless possibilities for careers. I like the strategy behind it and how every business decision really comes down to Finance. Beyond that, I am someone who does well with numbers but also taking them beyond that in a big picture understanding of what the numbers mean. Theology became an interest for me in school and it didn't take many classes to get a minor, I think the thought here goes beyond business and brings into question ethics in the business world, eventually helping me make moral decisions.

I would ultimately like to land in a role within consulting or mergers and acquisitions with goals of eventually working in venture capital or private equity. Problem solving is something I really have a knack for and enjoy taking part in anything that involves strategy. I like looking at the big picture to determine what makes the most sense in certain situations and why. In a job I want the opportunity to work hard and learn at a high level while absorbing as much useful information as possible.

Nidhi Ghorpade

nidhisg8@gmail.com

Wayne State University: Master's degree, Computer Science 2020

Pune Institute of Computer Technology: Bachelor of Engineering, Information Technology 2018

My name is Nidhi Ghorpade and this April I graduated from Wayne State University with a Master of Science degree in Computer Science. It was going to be the most awaited day of my life as I envisioned meeting my family after one and a half year and celebrating the big day with them. Little did I know that my plans were going to change in a drastic way. Master's degree at the age of 23 was my goal and I had done that because I remember seeing my parents' faces when I got into the best engineering college both happy and tensed as it was expensive to study in that college, but they promised to give me the best education and so I had promised them I will achieve all my goals and fill their lives with all the happiness that they deserve.

COVID-19 has affected me in a way where it is hard to wake up every day to hardly any possible job opportunities, rejections, and stress throughout the day. Every international student like me leaves their homeland to grow, work hard to achieve their goals and succeed making their families proud. It is a tough journey to be honest and it takes a lot to finish it, but the result has always been getting a dream job for each one of us. Summarily I would say it has been a roller coaster ride so far. I wake up with gratitude and positivity to apply for jobs and look out for any small or big opportunities that I can get, but sometimes it's just some calls and emails unanswered, job offer revoked because of COVID-19, not hearing back from recruiters or companies, rejections, being turned down because I am a recent graduate and then comes hope in the form of people reaching out on their own to help you in any way possible. And that is what keeps me going.

I am a computer science major who has always been passionate about technological evolution. I actively seek out new technologies and stay up to date on industry trends and advancements. In my recent experience with working as an Application Developer, I worked with the leading automotive and manufacturing industries to develop custom made forms and applications for them, enabling EDI. Proficient in development, using different programming languages and testing them, I have been able to play various roles throughout the whole software development lifecycle. Data and its beauty of visualization has always interested me and thus I geek out on Big Data and its technologies along with data visualization using intelligent BI tools. I have worked with gathering and maintaining data pipelines for large data sets along with building RESTful web applications and building ETL packages.

I have always worked on projects that could solve issues and provide best solutions. I am currently utilizing my time to teach a few Non-IT people programming languages like Python3. I designed everything about the course including content, video lectures, assignments, and quizzes. I am actively learning every day and I will use my potential to the best and not lose to COVID-19. I am looking for Data Engineer, Software Engineer and Application Developer opportunities in any field or industry because I am confident to be my best at whatever I do.

Nyjel Jackson

nyjeljackson7@gmail.com

Georgia Southern University: Bachelor of Business Administration, Business Management 2019

2020 started off for me, probably like many others, as the year I believed I would be able to hit the ground running, as I begin to start my young adult life. Back in March 2020, I had accepted an offer from GEICO Insurance Company, which was a program based on teaching and molding recent college graduates into future, successful leaders within the company; a leadership development program to be exact. With high hopes and eagerness to get started, I had to hit the brakes because of the emergence of COVID-19. The rise of this pandemic led the way for millions of American workers to be laid off/ let go, job offers rescinded, internships pulled, and others furloughed. Unfortunately I was one of those millions of workers. But let me give a little background, to when life was a little more "normal".

In May of 2019 I graduated with a B.B.A. in Business Management with a focus in Entrepreneurship, and a minor in Information Systems. While in school I worked as a Fitness Supervisor at our on-campus recreation center. What a fun time that was, and a great part of my college experience. In the summer of 2019 I would go on to accept an internship in the office of the Honorable Senator Johnny Isakson in Washington D.C. A friend of mine from school and I would go on to start with six other interns from the months of August to December 2019. Within a month's time I would be promoted to a Staff Assistant, and help run the daily office operations as well as assist in oversight of my once, fellow interns.

A lot of people would view working for an individual in Congress as working in politics, but I saw it as a wonderful opportunity to get a deeper understanding of how our legislative branch operates. This new insight would help me to learn the tiny things that go into the legislation process, and also to help me better serve my fellow Georgians/Americans from a federal government standpoint. In December of 2019, Senator Isakson would go on to retire from his position due to his progressive Parkinson's disease that he has been battling for some time now. Working for the Senator and temporarily living in the nation's capitol was a great experience to the start of my young life away from home.

Though my undergraduate degree is a business discipline, my curiosity has been drawn to multiple fields.

One can see that evidence through my pursuit of an internship with the U.S. Senate, as earlier stated. I have always had an interest to work in government (more so state or federal), business sales, data analytics, corporate finance/financial services, nonprofit work, and a slight curiosity for law, business and civil rights to be more exact. My industries of interest stem from different experiences I have had in my life, or from different courses I have taken during my undergraduate years, that draw my curiosity to them.

After I moved back to my home state of Georgia I began to apply to many different possible career paths in the private business sector. I eventually would land an interview with GEICO Insurance Company, and be offered and accept a position within their organization to start in April 2020. This puts us back to my original mention of trying to hit the ground running in the new roaring 20s, without the realization that it would be roaring at us; the whole world. The COVID-19 pandemic has made many of us wake up to the idea, that we do not have a full grasp over our life, and that plans can change in the blink of an eye. Plan for the inevitable is a saying I have been told for many years of my life. That is a very truthful statement.

Since my offer was rescinded back in April, I have been looking through public sector job postings within my home state, new career opportunities on LinkedIn, and simply going on company websites. This is in assumption that there is a position open that I might be interested in pursuing, or one that I would be eligible for through my knowledge and experience. I applied to a handful of companies, but I decided I did not want to blast my resume out as we all continued to wait to see if the job market would slowly pick back up or not. Gathering the encouragement and inspiration to put yourself out there, within the past two months, hasn't been as easy as one may think. Knowing that there are so many more individuals now, who are competing for viable positions, and understanding that they may have more experience and knowledge than you, can play on you subconsciously. Getting rejected is not the painful part. Honestly it's a learning experience. It's understanding that the resume, CV, and letters of recommendation, that you worked so hard to put together, can just not be good enough to get you in the door for an interview; before they can put the person to the paper(s). If that doesn't do it, then what will?

As of the present, I have been re-offered my same position with GEICO as I once had before. While I am very excited and grateful to be given this opportunity, I have to also be conscious of the matter to make a back-up plan. I say this because I want to be resilient, aware, and not ignorant to the fact that if another outbreak was to happen, I don't want to have all my cards on the table. I will continue my career search, while I wait for my new start date, for other possible opportunities that are equal to or greater than what I have now. I am not trying to be greedy, but I am cognizant that other doors may be opened if an unforeseen event impacts America once more. The Lord Almighty has truly blessed me with being able to share my story today, and to be able to pick back up on my young journey. One day, I hope to bring relief to the lives of many individuals who may be still recovering from our recent economic downturn. Only time will tell, but until then I will continue to rely on faith because that is the only thing no pandemic can take away from any of us.

Peter Hoang

peterhoangg@yahoo.com

University of Houston: BS, Mechanical Engineering 2020

Fall 2019 was the beginning of my senior year and I was looking forward to graduating college in May 2020. Like many other graduating students, I was trying to secure a full-time job in hopes of starting my career after graduating. Throughout the fall semester, I participated in resume reviews, mock interviews, networking events, company information sessions and career fairs to strengthen my chances of landing a full-time job. As a result, I was invited to interview in person with companies like ExxonMobil, Enterprise Products, Subsea 7 and Wood. After many rounds of interviews, I accepted a full-time offer from Subsea 7 in November 2019. I felt excited because of all the hard work I put into my academics and professional development throughout my college career. I felt like a burden was lifted off my shoulders because I had a job secured before graduating and that I could just focus on school.

In Spring 2020, I was completing my senior design project and wrapping up my final semester of college. I was definitely looking forward to walking the stage at my commencement ceremony and beginning my career as an Engineer. However, in April 2020, I received a phone call from Subsea 7 that they were going to rescind the full-time offer due to the coronavirus and the dropping oil prices. Just like that, I was back to where I was in Fall 2019 – back to searching for a full-time job. I was completely devastated because of all the hard work I put in to secure that full-time job. Ever since I had my job offer rescinded, I have been reaching out to recruiters on LinkedIn and applying to jobs online. It is an unfortunate situation for me, and everyone affected by COVID-19, but I am staying hopeful and patient because I am confident that I will be a valuable asset to a company.

I graduated Cum Laude from the University of Houston with a bachelor's degree in Mechanical Engineering and a minor in Mathematics. Industries that I am interested in working in include Aerospace, Aviation, Oil and Gas. I have over 15 months of internship experience from working as an engineering intern at TechnipFMC, United Airlines and Kroger. Currently, I am seeking a full-time mechanical engineering position.

Mentorship Journal

For the next 52 weeks, set up a meeting with a Mentor each week. In preparation for each week's meeting, write down a specific career goal, the progress made toward achieving the goal so far and your proposed strategy for achieving the goal. During the meeting, center the discussion on the predetermined career goal and achievement strategy. After the meeting, spend some time reflecting on the meeting discussion, write down the main takeaways and make any necessary changes to your career goal achievement strategy based on newly acquired knowledge from the meeting. Enjoy the weekly success skills word search puzzles along the way.

Accountability

CREDIBILITY DISCIPLINE ACCOUNTABLE
SUPERVISION FAIRNESS OPENNESS OBLIGATION
COMPETENCE HONESTY DISCLOSURE

W U R V W H O N E S T Y B E Z R
Y Q X X E G V H P K I K E R B X
B M N F J E O K A U S I N U N E
M I K N G Q T Z W A C Z I S V M
E L B A T N U O C C A O L O U W
S S E N N E P O I Z A U P L D Z
I F A I R N E S S E C U I C V C
Y T I L I B I D E R C H C S V C
L R N B Z E G P H E F U S I H Y
C O M P E T E N C E R E I D L J
G T J C L P D A G T Q J D J I Q
P C W K M Q Z A W D D B N T U F
O B L I G A T I O N P M X V P T
Y P C A I D K O N N B H S E B G
U A G A J D O Z Q F C T M W E B
S U P E R V I S I O N S X Q J T

Week 1

Meeting Date:

Mentor Name:

Career Goal & Achievement Strategy For Discussion

Meeting Reflections & Changes to Goal or Strategy

Adaptability

FLEXIBILITY AGILITY ABILITY RESPONSIVENESS
VERSATILITY RESILIENCE ROBUSTNESS
PERSISTENCE DURABILITY MANEUVERABILITY

E Y W D N N Q F Y P M B B W U Z
C T Z S D Q D D T Y S O G K Z S
N I H C Q V N Y I T T O S V A L
E L Q S Z O W T L I F C S B K C
T I V B Q X L I I L S F E S X Z
S B O X W L W L B I S E N A O S
I A M N Y R G I A B D S E M P O
S R R G R C X T R I N S V J Z N
R U B L W Z N A E X Y E I B P E
E D W P P I H S V E T N S N X U
P W P P N B N R U L I T N G P N
Y T I L I G A E E F L S O S V Z
M B G G G R I V N H I U P G L A
V E C O C E M N A I B B S M G N
L T N H C A Z T M K A O E O Z G
V E C N E I L I S E R R R F G E

Week 2

Meeting Date:

Mentor Name:

Career Goal & Achievement Strategy For Discussion

Meeting Reflections & Changes to Goal or Strategy

Agility

ENDURANCE	SPEED	DEXTERITY	MOBILITY
GRACEFULNESS	SKILL	BALANCE	RESPONSIVENESS
BRISKNESS	ALERTNESS		

S G J R A L P R Y N H A W T T N
S G H L N A S S E S B Q Q N M W
E R H B H L S A K O F C U O Z X
N A S Z Y A E P S I W V Q O A Q
E C E J T R N X A T X M V L S P
V E A A I K T H D F E D Q K B I
I F P I L G R R Y S K J I E B H
S U P W I S E S T I K L S E P S
N L V S B V L W I P L E S N Q G
O N T F O S A D R N O B E D J L
P E S G M D U L E X N J N U L K
S S M P F M E E T E U S K R M E
E S T H E K C G X R P M S A E L
R H D I W E O A E B E P I N H P
K J E T D K D V D S U N R C I V
W O B B A L A N C E F T B E C M

Week 3

Meeting Date:

Mentor Name:

Career Goal & Achievement Strategy For Discussion

Meeting Reflections & Changes to Goal or Strategy

Assertiveness

RESOLUTE	OPINIONATED	ENERGETIC	PROACTIVE
PRAGMATIC	EMPATHETIC	ASSURED	BOLD
STRONG-WILLED	OUTSPOKEN		

V D Z L S U S I E F K G T G V B
I U N M D U L U N G L A K I R V
J G Q E Y C Z Q D O Y P Y N X B
Y A O V O B I U L D X R Z Z F Z
O R Q I U O D D O E J A C T I M
H A K T T R C E B L F G I A O P
X C Z C S S C T D L W M T S S D
L I R A P J E A K I N A E S P S
E T P O O Q T N A W Y T H U R Y
S E Z R K S U O K G J I T R I P
B G Q P E X L I T N B C A E H Y
K R J O N C O N V O B P P D I S
D E M U O I S I Y R G J M Q T D
K N U T V C E P H T Q N E C F U
U E R B H P R O L S R C M T H C
I K Z E E M E S N X G M T T P J

Week 4

Meeting Date:

Mentor Name:

Career Goal & Achievement Strategy For Discussion

Meeting Reflections & Changes to Goal or Strategy

Authenticity

LEGITIMACY	CREDIBILITY	VALIDITY	GENUINE
VERACITY	ORIGINALITY	REAL	AUTHORSHIP
UNIQUENESS	INDIVIDUALITY		

```
I N D I V I D U A L I T Y M W T
L Q L L C V I N Z X G U W N I U
E O V M X L E G I T I M A C Y S
S Z K R W A A Y N K G K W X M P
R Z Z G E N U I N E J L A E R F
E Y O N C Z X Q A E Y Y P Y W P
P R A S V J C K T Z G U L A Y I
C R E D I B I L I T Y Z F S I H
V S P L U N I Q U E N E S S S S
Y E N N G E U F Q E T I F U H R
V R R U M G I X W Y L I G I X O
O J E A O R I G I N A L I T Y H
Z N N T C F C C D Z V Y M F U T
V A L I D I T Y P W J I Z L A U
Y M M O O U T G J J I D P T W A
V P J T L I J Y J V K O H V R Z
```

Week 5

Meeting Date:

Mentor Name:

Career Goal & Achievement Strategy For Discussion

Meeting Reflections & Changes to Goal or Strategy

Collaboration

PARTNERSHIP INTERDISCIPLINARY COACTION
TEAMWORK CONJUNCTION ENGAGEMENT
INTEGRATION ALLIANCE PARTICIPATION
ASSOCIATION

C E C N A I L L A K L T H I C I
L F A W H A B T K T H T V R E H
N O I T A R G E T N I N S K D R
P U I K V S Q R J P B E N W Y S
I T Q R K J A U R R P M O I A C
H A X O M G J J N U C E I M I K
S B A W U Y Q U Q O D G T U Y X
R V S M X D A T N K P A A Z J D
E V I A Q Z L J O T U G I S M C
N F S E Y V U F S K Z N C T R K
T H F T C N W W P S C E O J X I
R T B A C D G T L W J P S D M B
A V I T P H A X V U W Z S E Q D
P H I T J Z C L G F B K A D H R
N O I T A P I C I T R A P V U Q
N S A U E X B D N O I T C A O C

Week 6

Meeting Date:

Mentor Name:

Career Goal & Achievement Strategy For Discussion

Meeting Reflections & Changes to Goal or Strategy

Communication

MESSAGE LANGUAGE CONTACT MEDIA
INFORMATION TRANSMISSION TELECOMMUNICATION
CONNECTION INTERACTION CONVERSATION

J B F C O N V E R S A T I O N D

S O K H S H D M J R A W H G A Z

J T G O O C E E S G K G B P N T

B X M J I L S S T X T B J D O R

R T T Z V E R S H A U E O P I A

I D Z H U N L A K B L U Q Q T N

N X B H C N W G T D G S M O A S

T R S R Y F V E L I D Q F L M M

E J Z X N M Y K R I W Q Y I R I

R E H P E B V I T D W F I P O S

A Q R D O L Y X O A S D K G F S

C D I F Y A D Z V P A O M I N I

T A U S N L Z T C A T N O C I O

I N I R O N O I T C E N N O C N

O Q W E G A U G N A L G N E E G

N S S E Z S K E W T U G F Q B R

Week 7

Meeting Date:

Mentor Name:

Career Goal & Achievement Strategy For Discussion

Meeting Reflections & Changes to Goal or Strategy

Confidence

TRUST CERTAINTY HOPE MOMENTUM
ENTHUSIASM MORALE ASSURANCE AUTHORITY
EXPECTATION SENTIMENT

M J X V P T R M N Q E V A Q G D

S J X I K X W M X B W S W T W M

A M N A Z W M G Y Z S P N N U V

I Q O L M D I E K U Z H O E U A

S H X R F K R P R A M Z I M A O

U F I T A H I A W U O L T I E K

H L S R R L N U C T M D A T S S

T G V U Y C E O E H E L T N N A

N O L S E I U E R O N I C E Z F

E H D T L V Q U T R T V E S A O

Z L R Y E X C Z A I U E P D F A

C U R M O L A W I T M E X A L E

P L L W M Q T P N Y X P E K D Y

D F C R U I J I T A L O O F R H

X X S K Q H Q N Y E M H X R V L

H S L V Y X Y Z Z B L J B G D S

Week 8

Meeting Date:

Mentor Name:

Career Goal & Achievement Strategy For Discussion

Meeting Reflections & Changes to Goal or Strategy

Consistency

LOGIC ACCURACY COHESIVENESS UNIFORMITY
COHERENCE RELEVANCE INTERPRETATION
CONTINUITY STABILITY RELIABILITY

T	Y	W	C	O	H	E	R	E	N	C	E	F	C	X	S
N	T	H	V	K	U	O	Z	L	A	I	F	L	W	S	J
O	I	H	H	O	B	N	D	C	H	W	J	Y	E	Z	U
I	U	E	M	D	M	O	I	Y	F	Y	O	N	O	N	M
T	N	H	Z	X	E	J	M	F	R	W	E	F	Y	Z	J
A	I	N	Y	H	A	C	S	E	O	V	W	T	B	T	T
T	T	K	F	I	H	C	L	Q	I	R	I	G	S	Y	W
E	N	V	F	O	A	E	C	S	O	L	M	T	O	H	L
R	O	Y	X	R	V	B	E	U	I	B	A	I	P	J	L
P	C	V	A	A	W	H	O	B	R	B	N	J	T	P	J
R	Q	K	N	E	O	B	A	D	I	A	U	B	S	Y	L
E	I	C	V	C	T	I	E	L	F	Q	C	P	V	J	L
T	E	A	P	P	L	S	I	L	H	L	E	Y	P	O	F
N	X	M	T	E	Y	T	A	N	D	D	P	X	G	M	O
I	H	U	R	Q	Y	M	W	K	K	B	G	I	V	R	Y
D	Q	Q	S	O	R	N	F	I	L	A	C	T	B	C	R

Week 9

Meeting Date:

Mentor Name:

Career Goal & Achievement Strategy For Discussion

Meeting Reflections & Changes to Goal or Strategy

Cooperation

COMPETITION COORDINATION DEVELOPMENT
TRADE BILATERAL RELATIONS TIES DIALOGUE
AGREEMENT CONSULTATION

H L J A F K K F J H S K Y H T F
L I N O I T I T E P M O C T N Q
Y T D O V T C I G P R D M N E V
N X J Z A C X A Q G G D S E M S
V O H L C E R M M Q R N V M E I
F E I F V O T V W X O B G P E D
B N U T D R O Y S I T Y S O R H
I Y T G A N U R T D J D E L G T
L P G E O T P A D F O X I E A L
A S T M D L L I C I J E T V S T
T E G C W E A U V E N E O E E R
E H K N R V Q I S H G A N D Z A
R B C U N W R U D N R S T U E D
A U M V H U V Y J B O B A I Q E
L U W I D I R I W K U C K E O R
H W W G T X U N K G N J I G C N

Week 10

Meeting Date:

Mentor Name:

Career Goal & Achievement Strategy For Discussion

Meeting Reflections & Changes to Goal or Strategy

Courage

STRENGTH BRAVE PATIENCE HEROISM HEART
VIRTUE VALOR GALLANTRY NERVE
DETERMINATION

D J P V A L O R F L J G W J O P

Y F S P E E I O R K G Z Y K Q H

Q C H V V U H G E F W H L G I T

S U A R C E T A I V H S S X L N

F R E H U D G L E C N E I T A P

B N O T Q X N L S R A N N B J R

B B R W Y X E A X R W O B V N Z

E I U U P E R N U D I H M I I A

V P J G V B T T J F S I R K E C

M I U W J P S R F N O H J H P Q

P R J W L Z L Y A F J Q E T U Y

D E T E R M I N A T I O N A Z T

O W T T P F G Q R F T Y G L R B

V U W U T I D W N T F K Z U Q T

M M N D U H E R O I S M U A I R

N T W N X G H T U Y M G A C K U

Week 11

Meeting Date:

Mentor Name:

Career Goal & Achievement Strategy For Discussion

Meeting Reflections & Changes to Goal or Strategy

Creativity

VISION INNOVATION IMAGINATION INGENUITY
IDEA SOLUTION ORIGINALITY STORYTELLING
ARTISTRY INVENTION

N A R T I S T R Y E E L Q T Z W
O Y S C N V P D N W S S P A H M
I V Y U V X S R O P Y O F L T N
T F P X E E V S I B T R D A A O
A C F Y N C C S T D B A E D I I
N F E B T X T P A J Z V C A I T
I G O O I N W R V W O Z V L V U
G M A A O K B B O X O S O I V L
A Z X H N X I D N E D V S P D O
M N G H T A J E N A Z I A J E S
I H T P H E P R I F O J W I X E
C N U S S A D T Z N G P E O X W
O E O G V F X T A M T Z Q W B D
F E F D O R I G I N A L I T Y T
S T O R Y T E L L I N G Q D T J
Q U N K M I E Y T I U N E G N I

Week 12

Meeting Date:

Mentor Name:

Career Goal & Achievement Strategy For Discussion

Meeting Reflections & Changes to Goal or Strategy

Credibility

LEGITIMACY	INTEGRITY	ACCOUNTABILITY
LOYALTY	OBJECTIVITY	HONESTY
TRANSPARENCY	PERCEPTION	IMPARTIALITY
FAIRNESS		

Y R J V Z B F T G R N Q Y R E X
C M V J Q K G S R O O T V F V B
N P Q T D Y W L I H I S S F W J
E B B A F J T T J L V S R C C W
R T E Z Z E P I A Q E P S F P I
A Q D S J E L I V N I L F I J Y
P O X Q C O T E R I O V U R T M
S G D R Y R I I G Y T T Z I O J
N C E O A C A F A I Z C R J J O
A P A P A F W L C M T G E Z Q L
R K M M E H T W O J E I Q J X G
T I V E I Y H U U T V Y M T B V
Y T I L I B A T N U O C C A R O
N R D L U N H I E R E X I H C V
W R W W F A F Z P I X S H A N Y
Z J O D C H O N E S T Y R Y V Z

Week 13

Meeting Date:

Mentor Name:

Career Goal & Achievement Strategy For Discussion

Meeting Reflections & Changes to Goal or Strategy

Dependability

RELIABILITY	TRUSTWORTHY	PUNCTUALITY
THOROUGHNESS	DURABILITY	PRACTICALITY
RESILIENCY	ATTENTIVENESS	DESIRABILITY
	UNSWERVING	

Y G Z B R U Y W W T Y J A N E L
H S B Z X M C O I D N Y K I B C
T V C E S F N S H C T T V U E W
R Y R F O C E S S J S I T E R N
O T X F P W I E O S S L H D A D
W I D T X Y L N C R E A O J K U
T L U V H T I E A E N C A B N R
S I N J N I S V B L H I W H W A
U B S C W L E I W I G T M D L B
R A W B R A R T K A U C T E C I
T R E U R U V N Z B O A P K V L
D I R T T T J E S I R R K J A I
G S V U C C Y T O L O P M P P T
V E I H G N Z T N I H J A K W Y
F D N X O U N A A T T X Q B K Z
I N G A B P W A R Y Q F A X D V

Week 14

Meeting Date:

Mentor Name:

Career Goal & Achievement Strategy For Discussion

Meeting Reflections & Changes to Goal or Strategy

Diligence

DISCIPLINE	EFFORT	ASSIDUITY	SEDULITY
ATTENTION	PRUDENCE	HASTE	FORESIGHT
PROFESSIONALISM	ACUMEN		

E I M H Y X L V G C P A H B D O
Y M S B E J I M O L U S V F A A
Q F I G Z N X O H N G F F J S T
Z E L I D K I Q G W G I Z W E T
Z M A J S N S L F S C B J A E E
X S N S A P M G P Q R I Q Y C N
E G O T Q T S V A I B C S T N T
T F I L R R E J S U C H P I E I
S O S C P O A R S D R S A L D O
A R S P F F C F I Y L S I U U N
H E E A D F U A D P V E E D R P
Y S F N Q E M R U N V P P E P H
L I O K N V E X I A B T T S C K
P G R P S B N U T O I T P U N N
W H P N I W M F Y R P A Q U A P
E T R W U J Q N R X E R N L T J

Week 15

Meeting Date:

Mentor Name:

Career Goal & Achievement Strategy For Discussion

Meeting Reflections & Changes to Goal or Strategy

Elevator Pitch

PERSUASIVE	SPEECH	DELIVERY	APTITUDE
SPONTANEOUS	ASPIRATION	SUMMARIZE	VALUE
NATURAL	PRACTICE		

R X U S P I Z G V B X T A M A B
A N B S C K W F X F W P A P N L
R I H E C I T C A R P A Q E Q S
V D E L I V E R Y B H N Q X O U
A N E L R L R R W J L A J M M O
L T T D U Y T D N Z P T U H B E
U R I R B S P A Q B G U V I W N
E W Z I H I E L G S B R U K L A
E V I S A U S R E P A A N Y A T
Y S J G S O P J Y Q W L F X Y N
Q Z S U M M A R I Z E V P A K O
P X J A S P I R A T I O N L H P
W O Y M A G L Z O H C E E P S S
P E K X R E X K W K T B H C F R
G M C S W X C I Y G R A A K U C
J L G E D U T I T P A A B A C P

Week 16

Meeting Date:

Mentor Name:

Career Goal & Achievement Strategy For Discussion

Meeting Reflections & Changes to Goal or Strategy

Email Etiquette

PROFESSIONAL	THINK	SIGNATURE	SALUTATION
PROOFREAD	FONT	TONE	TRAIL	CONFIDENTIAL
INTERPRETATION			

E T J W E Q Y E U R M S P O K C
N O I T A T E R P R E T N I F T
U N J Y S M S X H M T U N R H P
O E Z R X U M A S W B Q O I I R
O N L F G D T I L B B N N U E O
H Z G F T P G U R U X K R A R O
T B Y R B N W Z N M T Q A T I F
G O A U A M M Z K S I A O W H R
Z I O T Y I C P S M A W T O M E
L T U U V D D L F R F A T I P A
P R O F E S S I O N A L W Z O D
E L A I T N E D I F N O C X R N
P E W U B B S U X Q Y E B Y C Z
T N O F F F S N D G F N R C Y B
D P M F P X P Y N F K Z J Z U M
W Q F G P T C J A W G L E O B E

Week 17

Meeting Date:

Mentor Name:

Career Goal & Achievement Strategy For Discussion

Meeting Reflections & Changes to Goal or Strategy

Emotional Intelligence

PAUSE	COMMITMENT	HELP	APPRECIATION
AUTHENTICITY	LEADERSHIP	AWARENESS	RESOLVE
GROWTH	RESPECTFUL		

Y L N Q Y O V P N B P Q Y P H P
T U T O V C W K W O B G L F D I
I F N H I A O G I Y M M U H J H
C T E E E T E H O M F E A E M S
I C M S M L A V X K N T T O V R
T E T H W B P I L O V V S A C E
N P I Y I R U D C O C T X J F D
E S M Q S B T H K E S Q S A G A
H E M T U N T F J X R E Y C U E
T R O M R W M W J W Y P R C S L
U R C I O I I D P Q S A P J C K
A V K R F M S H Z A Y F K A D H
W D G L A C D G Q D U Q P U H I
A Y A W A R E N E S S S N U P X
X Z W Y L E U F A N L F E N Y S
N Y N E O H B H R M W V Y L B F

Week 18

Meeting Date:

Mentor Name:

Career Goal & Achievement Strategy For Discussion

Meeting Reflections & Changes to Goal or Strategy

Empathy

COMPASSION	SYMPATHY	EMOTION	PERSPECTIVE
UNDERSTAND	ATTITUDE	INTEREST	COURAGE
CONVERSATION	MINDSET		

X D J Y C O U R A G E T J V E K
P E T H L M C W B U H Y R W B H
Y O P T V F G L L E J Z G Y L U
N F Z A U Y K E I C A Y M E N O
Q F S P N W N L Q M V J H V U L
I A E M D E D U T I T T A Y X C
A R Z Y E O Y G N N U R N T A D
A V Z S R J P G A E Z X O Y F P
N O I S S A P M O C T I I T Q X
Y W R P T P E R S P E C T I V E
W N Y A A T E S D N I M O F Z X
T S B W N X T R D U B U M S U U
M K W Z D Y S R T S E R E T N I
C O N V E R S A T I O N M S I N
N R M N K Y V E K D I X W Q Z U
O R H D G U U T Z V F X F N X O

Week 19

Meeting Date:

Mentor Name:

Career Goal & Achievement Strategy For Discussion

Meeting Reflections & Changes to Goal or Strategy

Entrepreneurship

INCUBATOR	INTRAPRENEURSHIP	VENTURE	CAPITAL
STARTUP	FRANCHISING	INVEST	OPPORTUNITY
BUSINESS	PLAN		

R J U M O R F F R M X Y H A C L
J C Z U W H I R E I P R Q E W H
D Q R G N I S I H C N A R F N O
R L O U V Z D L C A P I T A L P
I N T R A P R E N E U R S H I P
C J A X T G L U P E X G A Z X O
B N B O S S F A Z U J K H U U R
W J U S E X W H N Z T Z B B Z T
N Q C G V B D Z O F U R D P Z U
S G N M N Y M G I Q U K A O L N
V P I B I B U S I N E S S T L I
G G J R C L N Z K C M B P Q S T
S X A N E H E H M K W Q D I N Y
U C K N Q O J Z X M W Z V I F J
G U H M E R U T N E V O J P N K
C A K P M E R A K V Y B F G K K

Week 20

Meeting Date:

Mentor Name:

Career Goal & Achievement Strategy For Discussion

Meeting Reflections & Changes to Goal or Strategy

Goals

DESTINATION PURPOSE AIM INTENTION OBJECTIVE TARGET INTENT FINISH EFFORT OPPORTUNITY

Y O Q P V Y A G S X E K J P N F
T R N A Z G Y I Q J G Z S D O O
I F N D U R I B M U P J W I I T
N C R H G W S S H O A W M N T R
U I R K Z T E G R A T K E T A O
T Y Q H D A A I W M G I V E N F
R P P D H O V V T Q N S I N I F
O U W G E D A A S M F F T T T E
P R Y Q T S L X O H Z M C I S Q
P P D L R J T C S Y Q N E O E E
O O W P Q N Y I Y Y N M J N D Z
P S D S E A N O M O P X B F F N
X E Y T J I P A X B W O O B J D
T W N L F J C N H F T W J H G L
A I Y A I G W G O E W S K C W C
W I F Q Q D G O J H Z P T F L X

Week 21

Meeting Date:

Mentor Name:

Career Goal & Achievement Strategy For Discussion

Meeting Reflections & Changes to Goal or Strategy

Influence

IMPACT	GUIDE	SHAPE	AFTERMATH	HEART	LOGIC
PERSUADE	LEVERAGE	PROMOTE	BUILD		

Z V I W C C Z E N A D V M Q T F
R G T I W Q F G N A N N S N R S
Z K G I W P T U P Q A A G M A H
P O J R Q D R E K D R Z I X E A
L W T A Y X R O F S D I R E H P
X A R A F S A U M M B Y Z D C E
W D L P U T O F S O B K A I B K
K F Y A M K E S T P T X N U W R
B Z D L V T V R R W Y E I G I V
U E P T N C X J M T Q Y Y R D V
I W R C X T X L Q A B S C A A T
L Q B A X X U P Y K T Z C A Y W
D X F P K F T I Y L Z H X I T N
K H L M L W B K Z T E O F Y N Y
Q L U I N Y N E W E B Q I G M W
W S L E V E R A G E H S S L T Z

Week 22

Meeting Date:

Mentor Name:

Career Goal & Achievement Strategy For Discussion

Meeting Reflections & Changes to Goal or Strategy

Innovation

DESIGN COMPETITIVE CREATIVITY GLOBALIZATION
EFFICIENCY INVENTION TRANSFORMATION
IDEATION RESEARCH DEVELOPMENT

N V A N U I N V E N T I O N L Y

O U Y M O A G Y X G V E Y U G C

I Z B K Z I N G A L U U T D L N

T A G U X D T B H P X W I T O E

A D S B X U H A L G F V V K B I

M E O V C V O I E E R A I H A C

R V E T U O Z Y X D M V T F L I

O E T R O V M B S P I J A V I F

F L E E P T K P N G I S E D Z F

S O Q S K V T S E M H P R E A E

N P Y E W K Z N N T R M C H T D

A M H A W D N J D W I O G S I P

R E D R J E A K A P R T G Y O D

T N C C Z D K R V P E O I V N Q

H T V H U W F M P Z Z D V V V Z

L N J Y Y G Y B I T J E W L E B

Week 23

Meeting Date:

Mentor Name:

Career Goal & Achievement Strategy For Discussion

Meeting Reflections & Changes to Goal or Strategy

Integrity

ORIENTATION OBLIGATION TRANSPARENT
AUTHENTICITY PROBITY IMPARTIALITY VIRTUE
DECENCY SINCERITY ETHICAL

T	W	O	W	R	T	H	H	F	Y	L	Q	C	Z	J	J
N	Q	N	C	E	Y	G	F	L	T	A	F	R	H	I	A
E	P	O	M	T	D	S	L	J	I	C	X	E	S	B	N
R	Z	I	K	N	R	H	T	M	L	I	I	C	S	Y	M
A	S	T	Y	W	N	O	Q	W	A	H	D	V	A	T	A
P	L	A	A	Z	H	O	O	S	I	T	H	O	Y	I	B
S	N	G	Y	I	W	D	I	T	T	E	Z	Z	T	R	S
N	H	I	J	M	U	O	V	T	R	L	D	B	I	E	F
A	T	L	S	N	J	Q	K	M	A	X	O	M	B	C	N
R	P	B	Y	M	V	D	E	N	P	T	M	Y	O	N	Z
T	R	O	S	Q	B	C	X	U	M	L	N	V	R	I	W
A	U	T	H	E	N	T	I	C	I	T	Y	E	P	S	T
T	L	Y	V	E	A	V	P	Y	Y	Q	A	K	I	W	H
G	G	R	Z	C	D	S	K	G	C	P	S	G	L	R	G
T	N	U	F	X	M	K	M	W	P	W	D	J	U	Y	O
Y	C	N	E	C	E	D	W	E	U	T	R	I	V	Z	G

Week 24

Meeting Date:

Mentor Name:

Career Goal & Achievement Strategy For Discussion

Meeting Reflections & Changes to Goal or Strategy

Investment

STAKEHOLDER INTEREST INVESTOR VENTURE
PORTFOLIO ASSET FUND STOCK DIVERSIFICATION
SHARE

L R O U O E L G T T H R T D W E
V C B K C O T S C B P Q W C D R
B V L H M N P A L P A P B M I A
R O T S E V N I G O H I X E V H
G T P W J I U T E R N I G R E S
G V S G C B R K S T G S O E R Q
N Z F V M X U V E F I N F D S M
D T Z Q O Q E R D O Z Y M L I O
V N R U O N E N W L F H I O F B
C B T B T S S K Y I I S I H I Z
C M P U T P B M Y O U A P E C G
W T R A X F U N D H F D E K A F
H E X G C M Y J Q V C M S A T J
P Z V K L O G E Y K E P Q T I M
V I Y E B C I P R W Z S S S O P
G Y H Y C R F F J T E S S A N D

Week 25

Meeting Date:

Mentor Name:

Career Goal & Achievement Strategy For Discussion

Meeting Reflections & Changes to Goal or Strategy

Leadership

CHARISMA DIRECTION PASSION DELEGATION
INSPIRATION HUMILITY INTELLIGENCE RESILIENCE
PURPOSE EMPATHY

C W G P S H N C P Y M F Y B F I
E S V W S N H P X D W F F Y I S
S G Z S A F N D R V I P X Z C O
O E D T Q Y O U Y T I L I M U H
P C L Q P O I N O I T C E R I D
R N M I G E S F U V U I G W M A
U E C B T Q S D Y I N G W C P M
P I M S Q U A Y N S V D U Z C V
W L Q Q W H P Z P X G Z G N D W
P I V X O Q B I T Z W L P P H T
Z S J M I L R M A M S I R A H C
D E L E G A T I O N N H G A Q N
G R J J T D W Y E M X C V M U E
V Y W I F L D Y X Q O Y P F G U
Z E O Y H T A P M E N Y X A W V
I N E C N E G I L L E T N I C A

Week 26

Meeting Date:

Mentor Name:

Career Goal & Achievement Strategy For Discussion

Meeting Reflections & Changes to Goal or Strategy

Learn

ASCERTAIN DISCOVER TEACH PLAY PREPARE
EDUCATE UNDERSTAND DEVELOP ABSORB ASK

C D O P Q Q V X L T O I B G M S
S P N B G P D V E J E V C B G L
Q H H Y Z K Y V D X B A N E O A
A S C E R T A I N D G P C V D B
B J E O Y D D H E N D S E H I P
U W L T D A K S I A E B A T S Z
M D Z B Y E Y O Z T V J B T C K
Q K Y W E T X Y G S E A S Y O P
H F G M X A J M Z R L U O X V M
F P H U T C I Q W E O P R L E E
I K X T P U X C B D P V B W R H
H S S U Y D L J B N R P V A O Q
Z A T A N E S I M U Y E P M D F
P T L Q W B G T T S P E B N D K
Y P H O J C C J D J R U B W J G
Y X Y C E J Y P Z P Z M H H I C

Week 27

Meeting Date:

Mentor Name:

Career Goal & Achievement Strategy For Discussion

Meeting Reflections & Changes to Goal or Strategy

Listen

ATTENTION FEEDBACK NONJUDGMENTAL
CURIOSITY DIALOGUE MORE GAUGE INTENT
CONNECT BETTER

Y I D T N E T N I L T D Y J M M
F E E D B A C K N A G E U O S S
M G K A Q D E U G T P R R G B G
W K V T H P P G Y N A E T O Z X
B H X T K U C A Y E P Y E D K B
M T A E C J W U X M T T U H R O
N L R N O Q J G U G R I G N W T
M K T T N D H E E D J S O V R N
T Z C I N Y X O R U O O L V C H
C I Q O E B B G O J W I A G G M
B P C N C T E N R N D R I W P L
Y T M H T Y Y T E O W U D L T E
Y G U Z N M Q Q T N E C H X Y L
I U X U T K M H T C F W N D P S
A P K W K A G J E M Z J H V N X
W R B T O E T W B U P I H Y O E

Week 28

Meeting Date:

Mentor Name:

Career Goal & Achievement Strategy For Discussion

Meeting Reflections & Changes to Goal or Strategy

Loyalty

ALLEGIANCE	COMMITMENT	BOND	DEDICATION
DEVOTION	RELATIONS	HONESTY	RESPECT
SINCERITY	NURTURE		

B Z I N L M X C W W B Y A L R Q
Q G Q S T A Y I C C L Y X H E D
T N E M T I M M O C B Y X G S Y
Y F L Q A I V K M F G B O F P D
I T H Q S W T B V C F G L L E O
H I B N A Z P X O B O J T D C J
E R U T R U N T R N M H J E T K
V N N O X F N O Y L D A T V S M
B F D E D I C A T I O N Z O U S
V U U S N O I T A L E R R T J I
E C N A I G E L L A K O Q I C G
S G A L C W H T O U B D R O G E
R J U L S W S Y S J B G Q N O K
S W W E I E J Y T S E N O H P H
Z G I H J O Y E E O O G R Q R L
S I N C E R I T Y S Q G I T B Q

Week 29

Meeting Date:

Mentor Name:

Career Goal & Achievement Strategy For Discussion

Meeting Reflections & Changes to Goal or Strategy

Motivate

INSPIRE ENCOURAGE INCITE PROMPT ENERGIZE
CONVINCE MOBILIZE INSTILL INFLUENCE
EMPOWER

E X N U D Y Q Z R E D Z B G O I

E C T J U L L I T S N I H Q X J

W A N Y L X C I T P M O R P F H

R L O E O N C B Y P X Z Z B M X

E U R K U N Q X O F M Q Z T G U

W E E W I L M T W Z Z E T H C O

O A H N J A F N D X C M M E J W

P O Y J E B O N D N R O D N I G

M D Y E S R P D I K U B K C G O

E H Q R B A G V N W J I Q O N C

H D K I G F N I E T G L N U O N

R D I P C O K V Z H L I T R K O

A G B S C X N D E E F Z G A H W

J W Y N L N R I Z T W E X G E V

O K P I K K G R L R D W S E A E

S H Z H P W H T G R Z B M H W M

Week 30

Meeting Date:

Mentor Name:

Career Goal & Achievement Strategy For Discussion

Meeting Reflections & Changes to Goal or Strategy

Negotiate

BALANCE TERMS MEDIATE BARGAIN IMPROVISE
ARBITRATE INTERCEDE DEAL BIAS ART

R W C P W V T F B S S C A B Y M
H L U S D Q Z J L L X B I A S Z
M A P M E D E C R E T N I N G F
N E N E X W H S B N I A G R A B
A D S D T X U L M A K P H A X T
R P D I N D A V C R L U J Z T S
B W Y A S Z T Y Y B E A N V T P
I A D T V O Y R C A D T N K E C
T G T E Q V A A L W P Y T C W F
R V X I R R C Z J V A L O Z E M
A B G M S R E B T E I X I V Y N
T P L C F M X B M P J R T O L O
E Y K H D L L H I C G M K S V L
D Y T O M F R N C V L S Z M Q E
I M P R O V I S E S N G K R X N
B K E N P A R T T K A A A J P Z

Week 31

Meeting Date:

Mentor Name:

Career Goal & Achievement Strategy For Discussion

Meeting Reflections & Changes to Goal or Strategy

Network

MEET	CONNECT	CONTACT	ENCOUNTER	PROPEL
ENGAGE	HELP	OTHERS	EXCHANGE	RAPPORT

Y M T C O N T A C T K I B F M J
M L T E E M N P Z Y X D E X E C
X E Q M O E P T U M M H B C X O
Q P S U L G C K O G L T O A R B
Y O C A U A G T J X B H R H R V
Y R W S T J S W G A R X D T D W
L P E D C Y V I I F E G A G N E
U T N C O Z Y C A Q Z Y V E I R
P R C J N G G R S J U W F S J E
L O O F N K M R N F E N J V G H
E P U K E P E J J N T U S N V W
H P N R C H K R R D T M A L C T
X A T P T F H Y E A E H X D V R
W R E O T H L G U Y C T F W F F
A F R P S E F Z D X A M T O H D
T H A H O F W S E T Z L Y S S R

Week 32

Meeting Date:

Mentor Name:

Career Goal & Achievement Strategy For Discussion

Meeting Reflections & Changes to Goal or Strategy

Organization

ESTABLISHMENT INSTITUTION GROUP

MANAGEMENT STRUCTURE UNIT SOCIETY

INSTITUTION FORUM SYSTEM

O I X L H Z I Q F L M C Z W B K

J I R B N M P Y D N V Z S C I L

F I N S T I T U T I O N M Z H P

Z C F D Z U W R M S O B H N I E

Y R U U M E T S Y S M W N V C S

E S T A B L I S H M E N T F T L

N E N O I T U T I T S N I R X I

N Z H A I Y R M I H P N U J K L

L W A S L K C O O U E C W O P F

B X J T Q S G Q B E T P T E U Z

D S O C I E T Y X U Q Z C W O U

A O C W P D Z O R E Y I E Y R F

Y L J T N E M E G A N A M F G Q

L A V Y D F V C M U R O F T Y S

R X M W X Z G I V N A O M I H Y

J D L Y N S O T I N U A B Y P R

Week 33

Meeting Date:

Mentor Name:

Career Goal & Achievement Strategy For Discussion

Meeting Reflections & Changes to Goal or Strategy

Partnership

ORGANIZATION CONTRACT AGREEMENT
FRIENDSHIP VENTURE ALLIANCE RELATION
CONSORTIUM COMMITMENT STRATEGIC

```
P R N X N G F D J R F A Z K N D
I A T N E M T I M M O C E B K Q
H L N T J G C B Q R Q S A D E F
S L L M Y H Q S E I E G W P U D
D I O E E E O D S R R X E O G G
N A R L W J P F L E U Y C D X O
E N G G K C V U E K T T O O J B
I C A X M F B M V T H O N K C W
R E N W U Q E F C L J C S E T T
F H I Y W N D W A Z T U O J V T
G G Z K T G P Z U C H R R Y N T
W R A J I X B A Y Q J O T I T Q
F S T R A T E G I C C J I C E F
V P I T C A R T N O C S U Q A G
O S O P H W E X H V D L M D X Z
X J N H T E N O I T A L E R M X
```

Week 34

Meeting Date:

Mentor Name:

Career Goal & Achievement Strategy For Discussion

Meeting Reflections & Changes to Goal or Strategy

Performance

ACHIEVEMENT	CAPACITY	SERVICE	ENFORCEMENT
FRUITION	RESULT	EXECUTION	YIELD
FEAT	EFFORT		

U B P L X Z M F N J U E T I N T
T R M U M X F L G F B M R E R E
W G B K D U Q C N R L G O C N N
A R O L D P A O G A X U F I Q F
X P E H F N W Z Z C U C F V T O
I I N O R O D I R H P F E R L R
Y J O C U I K J P I L Z Q E U C
T O W U I T S X N E S S T S S E
Z H P A T U I R Z V U Q A M E M
D M C G I C G V N E W E E C R E
S S B N O E P D R M Y F F P A N
N H U K N X P I I E T X Q X I T
F K K K F E B K K N M I S Y K S
U V Z M N G L Z W T G O U R B I
L I G C A P A C I T Y Y S Z F W
J Y C V M O O L U P S X M S Z K

Week 35

Meeting Date:

Mentor Name:

Career Goal & Achievement Strategy For Discussion

Meeting Reflections & Changes to Goal or Strategy

Positive Attitude

ROUTINE	ATTITUDE	HAPPINESS	RELISH	SMILE
PROACTIVE	THOUGHTS	PURPOSE	ENTHUSIASM	ADAPT

F S V Q L S V E N I T U O R T C
M X H P H J A R D P K B O H O V
I A D N J D E D R V Z Y O D E G
C X J D A L U O L H K U R N W N
M Q G P I K A I A S G H T V A C
A V T S F C C T R H M H A C I O
H P H S T J T N T E U I X J Q J
A H I I K I L S G S N O L O S U
P X V S T C S A I V E D R E F I
P E S U Q W I A O S U Z D G J B
I L D D S F S D O K W J N C J O
N E J B K M R P J G C J Z N Q J
E M H D B D R F E C X C Y A J G
S A M I J U C F U O S I L O F C
S J N C P Z K N E G G J Y K H G
L W Z N Q Z B C Q E U Q F Z E A

Week 36

Meeting Date:

Mentor Name:

Career Goal & Achievement Strategy For Discussion

Meeting Reflections & Changes to Goal or Strategy

Problem Solving

DECISION BRAINSTORM OPTIONS CREATIVE
EXPLORE IDENTIFY DEFINE HEURISTIC
ALGORITHM TOOLBOX

A L G O R I T H M R Z I Z I K O
Z O J P Q Y C Y Z J W O S Z X O
A X P L D C N Q X H P L Z I H V
A K J R U H D D O W D H P Y H M
I E W Z S E H E B L S W G T R E
D L L E B U U C L D D J Z O D R
E M B E K R N I O S I P T D G O
N I I A Z I S S O V Q S C D T L
T F P I E S O I T B N R E K X P
I X L J D T S O U I E F B J F X
F S Q T E I X N A A I T Z U I E
Y H B C C C Z R T N Q X M N A K
Z U D S D G B I E W D A U E Q W
J F Q E M D V L X A L E M T H Y
L G K G A E U X I G Y S L U A R
Q P V U Q G K V S N O I T P O Z

Week 37

Meeting Date:

Mentor Name:

Career Goal & Achievement Strategy For Discussion

Meeting Reflections & Changes to Goal or Strategy

Process Improvement

QUALITY	CONTINUOUS	IDEATION	BENCHMARK
INCLUSION	SURVEY	IMPACT	AUTOMATION
METRICS	SCOPE		

H C Y Z M E T R I C S W R B U D
T Y W Z G U C F T A V D C I M X
G E G S E P Q X W H F C I W V T
S V Y B X V E V S X I E N F X F
L R B X L R I Y U U N O S B K X
F U Q M H P Q V O A V D I E I L
C S Q E Q O I R U X W T N N A G
F H Q F R G Y C N R S C C C U T
O Q K S M T Y G I Q X A L H T R
E S L S I E S J T R C P U M O T
T J M L R P T C N I I M S A M Z
E Q A W F O Q M O E P I I R A L
R U Z X Q C R Y C C P B O K T K
Q U H O R S F K W S Z G N X I L
K Q M M N O I T A E D I Y F O C
V X I H N X V E S P A I O X N Y

Week 38

Meeting Date:

Mentor Name:

Career Goal & Achievement Strategy For Discussion

Meeting Reflections & Changes to Goal or Strategy

Professionalism

EXPERTISE	COMPETENCE	SKILL	CREDENTIAL
QUALIFICATION	EXPERIENCE	PROFICIENCY	TALENT
EXCELLENCE	TRAINING		

M H F V E S I T R E P X E Q G X
N O W T G E V X R V B Y K W A Q
D C T Y I Q P J I A H N X I F Y
E C N E I R E P X E I I V F P V
T D E K S G Z Z A E K N C O S Y
R B Y N E H A S C U W Q I F B C
T U Z Q M W B N V O Z I O N F N
N X H P C R E D E N T I A L G E
E R E D B T R S J E P X A H W I
L F Z R E T M T E O N T O K W C
A O J P G J C S N L J G Q G U I
T C M G N K I G P X A U V B Q F
O O U L P V R H W V X H X I G O
C O W E G Q H C X G L L I K S R
N O I T A C I F I L A U Q S P P
E C N E L L E C X E F R K P D B

Week 39

Meeting Date:

Mentor Name:

Career Goal & Achievement Strategy For Discussion

Meeting Reflections & Changes to Goal or Strategy

Public Speaking

AUDIENCE REHEARSE FEEDBACK ENVIRONMENT
COMFORTABLE TONE EMOTION PACE
CONFIDENCE PROJECTION

N D A N D Y X N N F E E J F V I
O R G T I K C C O X S S E O Q J
I V O G X D O B B V R S C P Z A
T P X R G P M Q T P A P N A O P
C T L L P W F L C S E S E C F F
E W L Q T I O P J J H H D E Y T
J G Y C C I R M E K E O I H N A
O P O S A W T O C C R Y F W O T
R E V P P B A V N A J K N N I E
P W J O M Y B U E B H B O L T B
T N Y N O M L E I D Q G C C O Y
B J A Y L C E D D E T L W E M Z
X J Q P O U S N U E D H N V E S
O P G V O Z Y M A F X O F Q F D
A P F P N I I Z E M T P K F Z E
T N E M N O R I V N E Z B T D T

Week 40

Meeting Date:

Mentor Name:

Career Goal & Achievement Strategy For Discussion

Meeting Reflections & Changes to Goal or Strategy

Read

DECIPHER BOOKS GROW LANGUAGE INSPIRE
SKILLS MEMORY COMPREHENSION WORLDVIEW
LEARN

U U Q Z O T T Q P D B V L I X T
X U O W O E N B P L D X U Y X E
O E E W Y M L R E M E M O R Y K
N S Q G V C D A E G A L D E T P
B Y M A I B R I D H S L G A E D
I M T G N N O P N V P A Q U H W
O I C Y S Q R O T P U I I F U E
V S Q H P R Z F K G Z S C Z Q I
X A I B I Y I B N S N Y P E M V
J S G F R J Q A B V G M O N D D
D J I Y E A L M Q I S X K Y L L
C O M P R E H E N S I O N J Z R
R N Z I M O I X K B K X M E M O
X W S P O C W O R G M Q T R H W
Y N O O Q D U T F S A G P T U U
Z A S E S K I L L S U T N H S R

Week 41

Meeting Date:

Mentor Name:

Career Goal & Achievement Strategy For Discussion

Meeting Reflections & Changes to Goal or Strategy

Reputation

MISSION	PRESTIGE	ESTEEM	MARK	CACHET
CHARACTER	RESPECT	TRUST	DISTINGUISH	
ELEVATE				

H	Z	C	S	K	Y	T	U	M	O	Z	I	O	J	J	W
S	T	S	U	R	T	X	A	A	I	Z	D	M	R	I	B
I	Q	Z	C	R	V	R	V	L	G	C	I	O	F	C	G
U	T	P	F	A	K	I	I	Z	T	R	G	X	Q	D	Y
G	U	R	U	H	U	P	Q	E	Z	T	N	O	K	L	O
N	R	E	V	M	Y	U	H	F	C	H	Z	S	H	Z	M
I	I	S	R	S	A	C	J	E	W	N	H	P	J	I	V
T	A	T	M	N	A	X	P	P	O	N	N	Q	S	I	S
S	X	I	Q	C	C	S	V	C	B	V	J	S	U	N	J
I	V	G	Z	P	E	N	T	T	B	I	I	C	I	R	T
D	W	E	T	R	E	D	H	A	G	O	A	B	S	D	S
V	F	U	A	S	C	G	G	B	N	N	J	Z	I	Z	D
M	E	A	T	K	D	Q	V	R	B	J	D	W	Y	A	H
T	J	E	I	D	D	R	E	T	C	A	R	A	H	C	P
X	E	A	O	U	S	S	Y	Y	A	D	R	R	R	W	W
M	E	L	E	V	A	T	E	P	W	V	S	D	F	Q	I

Week 42

Meeting Date:

Mentor Name:

Career Goal & Achievement Strategy For Discussion

Meeting Reflections & Changes to Goal or Strategy

Research

KNOWLEDGE	INVESTIGATE	EXPERIMENT	REVIEW
EXPLORE	DISCOVERY	SURVEY	ANALYSIS	INQUIRY
METHOD			

B H Z G W G T C N F R T B B G V
M J E C U S T P B W A T Q E W O
F R X M S W C Y W X D A I E W V
R K P E A Z Q R I K A R I A Y M
N A E K Z M P I B E T V M R E J
K E R I T M R N E V E W E T T K
Q G I N Q K B V G R X V H A P P
P D M Q Y D G E O I O O Q N T S
B E E U H S E S C C D V Z A U H
O L N I H E T T S A H U E L K S
W W T R G C X I U R N S X Y C C
Z O W Y H U D G D M K U P S V I
O N A U X B Q A I D M R L I S W
O K J E P L U T S J Q V O S Z U
I S T K N K P E S I U E R Y E P
N T J X V R O Q F B V Y E X N F

Week 43

Meeting Date:

Mentor Name:

Career Goal & Achievement Strategy For Discussion

Meeting Reflections & Changes to Goal or Strategy

Respect

CHARACTER	HONOR	ESTEEM	VALUE	HOMAGE
DIGNITY	RECOGNITION	APPRECIATE	REVERENCE	
ACCLAIM				

Y L E U L A V H E B R R R U L L
J K X C G X F E G A M O H N X A
G N R R P R C H A R A C T E R P
U X X G O R V K T T H S F S E P
E R G N Y N H V B Z L E V P C R
Y C O S X S H P N X I N L M O E
A H N O K M S P Z D G H C A G C
F I S E W H Q J X Z T X S E N I
O Y M A R D N H Y X Y D V O I A
A M H C T E I B W Q M T L W T T
Y X B C O E V G I R Z E P R I E
D O E L K B S E N O A O B Q O Z
P H K A S K T T R I A H J J N S
L B P I G H A L E R T S N T A Q
O F O M V S X D E E P Y J D T Q
D L I K B B V L A K M F L S E J

Week 44

Meeting Date:

Mentor Name:

Career Goal & Achievement Strategy For Discussion

Meeting Reflections & Changes to Goal or Strategy

Risk Management

ROBUST CONTEXT ANALYSIS EVALUATION
CONSEQUENCE MITIGATION ASSESSMENT
COMPREHENSIVE THREAT RESOURCE

D C O M P R E H E N S I V E N W
D D B T J V P B N A I M X K O U
E I H S Z C E R E X N B S T R X
Q C W R F Y O Z H H T G I V Q S
O N R X O P G N U A E S S E J P
F I W U G B E F T A A Z Y V A I
C H D N O O U A S E L D L A J U
G D S Z E S R S R N X K A L Q B
W O V N Y B E U T H U T N U R W
K T D A S S C R G A J F A A D B
F V W O S F E W R D J P I T X G
T C F M G R C F A Y V R U I B V
C M E Y T C Y I H O G A Y O F K
H N K W M I T I G A T I O N B P
T O E C N E U Q E S N O C N B B
E X Q W M U F N G T A E R H T X

Week 45

Meeting Date:

Mentor Name:

Career Goal & Achievement Strategy For Discussion

Meeting Reflections & Changes to Goal or Strategy

Strategy

TACTIC	SCHEME	PRIORITY	APPROACH	FOCUS
OBJECTIVES	PLAN	INITIATIVE	CONCEPT	AIM

C O N C E P T A P P R O A C H S
K X B A R A Y D C J Y J W C C K
O H E A P I N I T I A T I V E Q
U B D P L U M V J C S J Y Z A T
S Q J G A A F U K L E X H N T N
C N P E N Y J V H I I S U C O F
H J Z R C K D E Z B T M I A P Q
E Y N B Y T F O Y A L N D T C G
M O B G S S I V S T G I X U I I
E Y D J Q L G V N T O I J U T L
F A A P H L Y A E R E B S O C U
Y D G V D O C B G S G Y F B A E
C E S Y D R S A E N L M A N T H
H J T D C W A L Z O K V Y R G J
F U C P R U L N Z B L I P X G L
P T A S O Q E P Y T I R O I R P

Week 46

Meeting Date:

Mentor Name:

Career Goal & Achievement Strategy For Discussion

Meeting Reflections & Changes to Goal or Strategy

Team Work

COMPELLING DIRECTION STRUCTURE SUPPORT
CHALLENGES DYNAMIC DIVERSITY ENGAGE
CONSEQUENTIAL RECOGNITION

```
T X N Z H B E Y A A I F J Z E B
E C O H A C H A L L E N G E S Q
R W I O Q H S N O I T C E R I D
U D T J S W O Y T I S R E V I D
T C I K B S W E C J O N R T J Y
C O N K K J Y D A B G Q H Z E S
U M G R P S G D D A T D Q U C R
R P O X E D M Y G I R J Z U C Q
T E C K T N N E G X O F S U G P
S L E L K A L N L I P K I C B O
L L R W M C G J U C P M V A L T
P I L I S H S U S L U W E J L C
U N C O S O I P H U S R G G J Z
G G L A I T N E U Q E S N O C D
C E Q F M G F O I O F Z I D Q W
L X Q S T R G U I T F B F Y G L
```

Week 47

Meeting Date:

Mentor Name:

Career Goal & Achievement Strategy For Discussion

Meeting Reflections & Changes to Goal or Strategy

Technical Literacy

CHANGE	SIGNIFICANCE	EMBRACE	REVOLUTION
BLUEPRINT	COMPETENCE	CRUCIAL	UNDERSTAND
CAPACITY	TRADEOFF		

G M U N D E R S T A N D N D Q X
E U P N J R A D K E L U F C W F
T N I R P E U L B I F W P R B Q
B G I G Z D W L S I U Y A H A A
A Z H B R Z M X X D B W R H R X
B J A B I H N F F O E D A R T P
E C N A C I F I N G I S W Z Y C
E D W F S Y W N S F G A G H D O
S M U X X R E V O L U T I O N M
C R U C I A L E N Z P Y J Z A P
P L Q X Z Y D U Y O Z Z E V F E
H O S D P E X J Z I Z U W P V T
L B G Y T I C A P A C F B K C E
F X H B B L Q E G N A H C Q Q N
M N T B K D S G E T X T Q F N C
W P M E C A R B M E S M B W E E

Week 48

Meeting Date:

Mentor Name:

Career Goal & Achievement Strategy For Discussion

Meeting Reflections & Changes to Goal or Strategy

Tenacity

PERSISTENCE PERSEVERANCE GRIT PERTINACITY
DETERMINATION DECISIVENESS FORTITUDE
STEADFASTNESS RESILIENCE POISE

V	T	D	W	H	U	S	Z	T	E	Y	Y	D	K	C	R
R	D	T	P	Y	M	V	D	N	T	P	E	Z	K	W	F
E	G	T	H	I	D	Y	K	I	E	T	N	S	B	E	P
P	K	Q	F	W	D	J	C	D	E	T	T	N	B	E	Z
V	Z	J	C	G	P	A	U	R	C	I	J	C	R	U	Q
K	O	E	T	I	N	T	M	F	E	R	W	S	H	P	P
A	T	O	B	I	I	I	Y	Q	E	G	I	J	I	V	O
W	Q	I	T	T	N	Y	H	L	O	S	E	P	D	J	I
W	K	R	R	A	K	M	U	W	T	B	Z	V	W	G	S
V	E	O	T	T	E	N	T	E	Y	X	E	E	X	L	E
P	F	I	Y	P	C	F	N	F	I	R	K	O	Z	Z	E
Z	O	R	O	I	P	C	A	W	G	O	F	Z	W	O	Y
N	Q	E	C	N	E	I	L	I	S	E	R	E	S	E	L
D	T	X	I	P	E	R	S	E	V	E	R	A	N	C	E
I	J	I	V	S	S	E	N	E	V	I	S	I	C	E	D
S	T	E	A	D	F	A	S	T	N	E	S	S	X	K	K

Week 49

Meeting Date:

Mentor Name:

Career Goal & Achievement Strategy For Discussion

Meeting Reflections & Changes to Goal or Strategy

Time Management

TIME CONTROL EFFECTIVENESS EFFICIENCY
PRODUCTIVITY METHOD TRACK LIMIT MINDSET
MANAGE

S P R O D U C T I V I T Y G I B
S U F C Q E T M O U X F Z R L L
E M R U Y I O X I J F L X A P M
N K W Y M C Z P B N S Y S U J B
E O E E L T N Y U D D J Q L T B
V L K E S B M E L O O S Q W I D
I G X O R S O V I M O H E U M S
T G T U G I J J K C A I T T I N
C K E V F U V L E L I N B E L A
E C K P M S O D T X D F A L M A
F A F S S R J V J E N H F G C M
F R R H T U S T Q X S B A E E W
E T K N C S X N I E L J F W C H
Y Q O R U O N Z V R U W X A W A
N C V P T F F D V J M J F C Q I
Q T Q Q X U D A R E P N K N A Q

Week 50

Meeting Date:

Mentor Name:

Career Goal & Achievement Strategy For Discussion

Meeting Reflections & Changes to Goal or Strategy

Work Ethic

TRUST	RESULT	INTEGRITY	DEDICATION	FOCUS
DETERMINATION	DISCIPLINE	RESPONSIBILITY		
PUNCTUAL	PREPARATION			

X Y E W D Q G V F K V E H O T B
P T M K R E N I L P I C S I D Y
T H O Y U P D Z B C T U F M W S
J L M S T C G B H O O X N R Z T
R F S X L T H P X Z O U S H M W
J O K K U S C E L D P K A K G R
B C X V S U I G Y F I B Z O Y M
P U P Z E R T J B A Q R R T Y M
T S U N R T N O I T A C I D E D
H R T N O I T A N I M R E T E D
I U G U C R K R H B G C H T H L
F N O I T A R A P E R P Q H E P
L U X Q P R A B T K J X O C U E
Q G I V D X P N Z G F O T P L K
Y T I L I B I S N O P S E R D S
P U N C T U A L E L W Y H A U H

Week 51

Meeting Date:

Mentor Name:

Career Goal & Achievement Strategy For Discussion

Meeting Reflections & Changes to Goal or Strategy

Work-Life Balance

VACATION TIME PRIORITY FAMILY EXERCISE
WORK SCHEDULE FLEXIBLE HOBBY BURNOUT

V E L C Z P R I O R I T Y T G K
D T F F Z U C K O V J N M T L E
N B C W O G A H G M O F I Z S C
F S G O D K H I X I Y C V I X Y
M I V E Q V N S T K V D C I M H
X M B B L K H A F K K R V I W D
M R G U N U C H M N E F M T Q W
M P Y C R A D R B X X W E M I T
F A E L V N P E E S K K I Y T D
G L P S I P O A H K T K N U E N
W H E O L M B U R C K L Q B T X
Q I B X V Y A O T G S R L I Z U
Q V L A I B W F C O P N L U F O
Q A K E W B Y G L X T K S D W R
U A O K E O L U L H H D B T P Q
T K D C Y H U E A U A R L O C K

Week 52

Meeting Date:

Mentor Name:

Career Goal & Achievement Strategy For Discussion

Meeting Reflections & Changes to Goal or Strategy

Congratulations on completing 52 weeks of mentorship. I hope by now you have a solid strategy in place for leaving your mark professionally. I also hope the process encourages you to make an impact in other lives by being a Mentor in return. Enjoy the journey along the way as you continue building genuine relationships through Mentorship. Wishing you a bright and fulfilling future ahead!

Made in the USA
Middletown, DE
20 September 2022